D1035713

Becoming a Feminist

By the same author

Feminism and Family Planning, with J. A. Banks
    (Liverpool University Press, 1964)
The Sociology of Education (Batsford, 1968)
Faces of Feminism (Martin Robertson, 1981)
Biographical Dictionary of British Feminists, 1800–1930
    (Wheatsheaf Books and New York University Press,
    1985)

Becoming a Feminist

The Social Origins of 'First Wave' Feminism

Olive Banks
Emerita Professor of Sociology
University of Leicester

The University of Georgia Press
Athens

Published in the United States of
America in 1987 by the
University of Georgia Press
Athens, Georgia 30602

ISBN 0–8203–0914–1
LC 86–16129

Phototypeset in Linotron Times
by Input Typesetting Ltd, London
Printed and bound in Great Britain by
Biddles Ltd, Guildford and King's Lynn

Table of Contents

1 Introduction

The study of what is coming to be called 'first-wave' feminism (Sarah 1982), to distinguish it from the modern women's movement, is now an established part of women's studies, and, if it is still largely neglected by male historians, it has been well served by a number of female scholars, who have explored in depth particular aspects of feminist history (Taylor 1983, Liddington and Norris 1978, John 1984, Rendall 1985, Lewis 1984, Walkowitz 1980). What has so far not been attempted has been a systematic study of the feminists themselves. This is not to suggest that biographical material has been ignored. It has been used extensively and imaginatively by historians in an attempt to understand certain phases of feminism and, at the other extreme, there have been a number of biographies which have increased our awareness of the contribution of particular women to the women's movement (Rowbotham 1977, Liddington 1984). At the same time the recently published first volume of the *Biographical Dictionary of British Feminists* (Banks 1985) has brought together information on the lives of both women and men who were active in the women's movement between 1800 and 1930, and so provided the basis for a life-history approach both to the feminists themselves and to the movement they created.

The data on which this study is based is, therefore, mainly biographical in nature although the method of analysis is primarily sociological. Making use of the same sources as the *Biographical Dictionary*, work on both the Dictionary and the present study in fact proceeded concurrently. They also make use of virtually the same sample although the

1

final products are very different in both form and content. Readers of this study will find very little biographical detail, although certain individuals have been used as examples, and readers looking for such detail are referred to the Dictionary. On the other hand, the format of the Dictionary necessarily precluded any but the most superficial attempt at analysis, and it is this analysis which the present study attempts to provide.

It is necessary, at this stage, to describe the manner in which the entries to the Dictionary were chosen since this has crucial implications for the present study. Feminism, like socialism, is in many ways impossible to define in any really objective way so that, in the last resort, the choice of entries is, and must be, a very personal one. In general, however, the aim has been to adopt a wide rather than a narrow definition of feminism, and one which accords with the thinking of 'first-wave' feminists, rather than feminism today. In other words, an attempt was made to set the definition in its historical context although, where appropriate, comparisons have been made with the modern movement and both similarities and differences drawn out. The main guiding principle which has been used to make the selection is the presence of a critique of the traditional subordination of women, enshrined as it was in law, custom and religion, and a claim for a new relationship between men and women which would give women greater control over their lives. Within this framework, however, there was room for a great variety of positions with respect both to the nature of the critique itself and to the kind, and especially the extent, of the changes which were believed to be necessary. An attempt was made, very deliberately, to reflect these differences in the selection of entries.

Another decision which influenced the nature of the selection of entries was that it should be a Dictionary of feminist activists rather than the very much larger number of individuals who might be described as feminist sympathisers. Those included in the Dictionary, therefore, and consequently included in the present study, had all been involved actively in one way or another in working for the attainment of feminist goals. For this reason a number of men and women who were certainly feminist in ideology but who gave their lives to other causes have been excluded. Eleanor Marx, for example, was certainly a feminist by inclination but chose to commit herself to socialism rather than feminism. There were also a number of women who, like Beatrice Webb, were decidedly ambivalent towards the women's movement. Some of these, like Beatrice Webb herself, have been excluded but others, like Florence Nightingale and Caroline Norton, have been considered sufficiently important within the women's movement to have been included.

Another kind of difficulty in selecting entries for the Dictionary, and which pressed with even greater severity on the present study, was the lack of biographical information available for women generally. They appear less frequently in biographical dictionaries and are of less interest to biographers, so that without the recent interest taken in them by feminist scholars many names would have been absent from both the Dictionary and the present study. This is particularly true of working-class feminists and of women whose activity was confined to the local rather than the national level, and it may well be that such women are under-represented in the study, although every effort has been made to include as many as possible.

Another decision which may appear to some readers as contentious is the inclusion in the Dictionary of a small number of men who were active in 'first-wave' feminism. They have a special significance for the present volume, however, since to uncover the process by which a man becomes a feminist would seem to pose even more complex and interesting problems than to ask a similar question of a woman. To emphasise this difference the male sample has been given a chapter to itself, and the main analysis is of the female sample only.

The entries in the Dictionary and, consequently, the sample of feminists which make up this study, cannot claim to be based on a truly objective definition of feminism or feminists. Nor can it make any claim to completeness. Indeed it is difficult to see how such a claim could be fulfilled. The conclusions of the study therefore are based only on the sample itself, a full list of which is given as an Appendix. If, however, it is prudent to recognise the limitations of the sample, it would be wrong to assume that it is in any sense random or arbitrary. It certainly includes the great majority of the leaders of the women's movement during the period of the study as well as its most active supporters and it is women, and men, on the fringes of the movement who have presented problems of selection, either because their status as feminists was in doubt (as in the case of Eleanor Marx), or, much more frequently, because there was inadequate information to include them.

The final sample contained 98 women and 18 men. This is three less than in the Biographical Dictionary, because in these cases the information available was judged inadequate for the purpose of the present study. Neither sample is very large, but the group of 98 women is of sufficient size to make possible a simple quantitative analysis, and it is this analysis which makes up the bulk of the study. The male sample is too small to analyse in the same way, but makes it possible to examine both the difference between men and women feminists and the role that men have played in the women's movement.

Throughout the study as a whole the main unit of analysis has been the cohort or generation, based on year of birth. Four cohorts have been designated, cohort I consisting of all those born before 1828 and so representing the first generation of the women's movement. Active, in many cases, even before there was an organised movement, it includes pioneering women like Caroline Norton who, born in 1808, successfully stage-managed the first piece of feminist legislation in 1839 (Holcombe 1983, Forster 1984). Other significant feminists in this cohort include some of the earliest pioneers in the education of girls, like Anne Jemima Clough, Frances Mary Buss and the two Shirreff sisters, as well as most of the Owenite socialist feminists like Anna Wheeler and Frances Wright.

The second cohort were born between 1828 and 1848 and this covers most of the leaders of nineteenth-century feminism once it had emerged as an organised social movement. It includes, for example, both Elizabeth Garrett Anderson, born in 1836, and Sophia Jex-Blake, born in 1840, who between them pioneered the opening of the medical profession to women (Manton 1965, Todd 1918), and Emily Davies, born in 1830, who did perhaps more than anyone else to open higher education to women (Stephen 1927, Forster 1984). Several nineteenth-century suffrage leaders also fell into this cohort, including Helen Blackburn, Ursula Bright and Millicent Garrett Fawcett. It also includes Josephine Butler, born in 1828, a feminist of wide sympathies best known for her work in opposition to the Contagious Diseases Acts (Walkowitz 1980, Spender 1983).

Those in the third cohort were born between 1849 and 1871 and came into the women's movement only during the last decades of the nineteenth century. By this time the suffrage issue had begun to take precedence over all else and it is this cohort therefore that provided the leadership of the suffrage movement as it moved into the twentieth century. The most important women in this group included the militant leaders Emmeline Pankhurst and Emmeline Pethick-Lawrence, as well as the courageous Constance Lytton who became one of the movement's martyrs (Lytton 1914). By no means all the women in the cohort were militant however, and on the constitutional side it included Helena Swanwick, Isabella Ford and Frances Balfour.

Cohort IV, born between 1872 and 1891, represent the last generation of 'first-wave' feminism. Most of them were caught up as young women in the suffrage campaign, which now dominated the women's movement, and some of them, like the two Pankhurst sisters Christabel and Sylvia, were amongst its most important leaders (Mitchell 1967). It was this generation however which saw the partial success of the suffrage campaign in 1918, and its final success in 1928, and it was the way in which this cohort responded to their victory which provides a way of understanding what happened to feminism in the years after the First World War.

The cohorts have provided the basis for the analysis, in Chapter 2, of the social background of the female sample. For this purpose the social origin, educational qualifications, religious affiliation and political affiliation of the sample, in so far as these were known, have been analysed in relationship not only to the cohorts themselves but to each other. This information not only gives us a more detailed picture than was previously available of who, exactly, first-wave feminists were, at different periods of time but, even more significantly, points up the changing political affiliations of the feminists themselves and, in consequence, those of the feminist movement.

One of the intensions of the study as a whole was to examine the extent to which feminist beliefs reflect childhood experiences, especially with parents, but unfortunately this was the area in which gaps in the information available was most painfully obvious. Wherever possible, however, an attempt has been made to provide a relatively simple classification of mother/child and father/child relationships in order to explore the extent to which feminism can be seen as a reaction against or a response to experiences within the family. Necessarily, because of the lack of information in this area, the picture is very far from complete, but it is more systematic than any previous attempt to explore the childhood roots of feminism. The same chapter looks at marriage as a causal factor in feminist attitudes. Many of the women in the sample remained unmarried all their lives and others married only in late middle age so that it was possible to compare married and unmarried women in terms both of their involvement in the feminist movement and of their feminist ideology. The kinds of marital experience were also analysed in the same way in order to explore the different consequences of an unhappy and a happy marriage. Perhaps the most surprising finding of this aspect of the analysis was the extent to which the feminists, sometimes perhaps unconsciously but often consciously, sought a husband who shared their view, while others, fearing the effect of marriage on their freedom, avoided it altogether.

The main justification for the present study is its methodology which by examining the lives of individual feminists makes possible an exploration of the way in which personal experiences interact with ideological perspectives and indeed with the level of commitment to feminism itself. This is made possible by the analysis in Chapters 4 and 5 of the involvement of the female sample in both feminist campaigns and feminist ideology in terms of their social background and religious and political affiliation and in terms of their family relationships. Of these, political affiliation appeared to be the most significant, and one of the most striking findings of the study, which emerges as one of its major themes, is the extent to which 'first-wave' feminism not only changed the nature of its political affiliation at some time towards the end of the nineteenth century, but in doing so changed, in a fairly dramatic way, the whole nature of feminism itself.

Another major concern of the study has been to throw further light on the argument advanced in *Faces of Feminism* (Banks 1981) that feminism encompasses three different ideologies, which in many respects are not only different in their emphases but may even be contradictory. By adopting a different methodology it was hoped to assess, with much more accuracy than before, not simply the existence of these different traditions but the relative importance of each in contributing to the development of the women's movement, and the way in which this changed over time. The major tradition was defined as equal-rights feminism, with its roots in the Enlightenment, which was given theoretical justification in Mill's *Subjection of Women*, published in 1869 (Rossi 1970). The second tradition came from the evangelical movement and, while it inspired many women to an awareness of the limitations imposed on them by their subordinate role, rested its case not on any doctrine of human rights but on the need to give women's special and unique qualities more significance in public life.

The third feminist tradition, socialist feminism, developed initially within Owenite socialism and shared with Owenism a belief in a radical change in family life which would free women from both domestic slavery and legal and political subordination (Taylor 1983). This version of feminism did not survive the decline of communitarian socialism in the 1840s but was replaced at the end of the nineteenth century by a new socialist feminism which, much less radical than Owenite feminism, placed its faith not on communitarianism but on the development of the welfare state.

The main way in which the present study can explore the relative significance over time of these three traditions is through changes in religious and political affiliation and these reveal both the presence of different political and religious ideologies and significant changes over time. The most remarkable of these is the way in which by the begin-

ning of the twentieth century the nineteenth-century dominance of the equal-rights tradition had been largely replaced
by socialist feminism, with quite crucial consequences for
feminism itself. Thus differences in religious and particularly
in political affiliation can be demonstrated to be related
both to feminist involvement in particular campaigns and,
even more strikingly, to aspects of feminist ideology.

So far the analysis has been concerned only with the 98
women in the sample. The 18 male feminists are, for a
number of reasons, examined in a separate chapter. With
such a small total the analysis is also much less precise. The
general framework, however, follows the same pattern as
for the women, making use of the same categories and the
same method of analysis in so far as numbers allow. The
material, moreover, in spite of its limitations, gives a clear
picture of who the male feminists were and the general
nature of their involvement in the women's movement. The
comparison over time, using the same time periods as in the
case of the female sample, also makes clear that men began
to withdraw from active involvement in the women's movement even before the goals of suffrage had been attained
and that male interest in feminism was in fact a characteristic
of a Liberal rather than a socialist political affiliation.
Indeed, one of the arguments to be made in this and other
chapters is that, on the whole, modern socialist thought
whether Marxist or non-Marxist has had little sympathy for
the goals of feminism, in spite of the attempts of socialist
feminists to draw them together. In assessing the role of
men in the women's movement, therefore, the discussion
takes account both of the nature and extent of men's contribution to 'first-wave' feminism and their limitations as
feminist allies.

The main analysis for both the female and the male
sample is now complete and it is possible to turn to what is
in fact the central theme of the study, the process of
becoming a feminist. Two different mechanisms in this
process are distinguished; a reaction to a personal situation
of despair or frustration, and a response to an intellectual
tradition of social and political reform. Consideration is
given, in both these contexts, to the significance, for both
the female and the male sample, of social networks both in

drawing women and men into the women's movement and in keeping them there. In the same connection attention is paid to the kind of charismatic leadership provided, for example, by the Pankhurst family, as well as to what might be called the collective enthusiasm inspired above all by the drama and sacrifice involved in the militant suffrage campaign. Some of the implications of these findings are then used to throw light on the decline of feminism after 1930, as well as its re-emergence in a somewhat different form during the 1960s.

In choosing to emphasise the process of becoming a feminist the study has attempted to draw attention to the extent to which active involvement in the women's movement was, even for the most conservative of feminists, a conscious and deliberate act of revolt, even if it was only a revolt against the current belief that intellectual pursuits were harmful to girls and women. At a time when current research emphasises above all else the strength of the forces which impose traditional ideas of gender on both girls and boys even at the present day, it is surely both useful and encouraging to understand something of the process which in the past allowed women, and sometimes men, not only to reject these ideas but embark actively upon the hazardous process of trying to change them.

In arguing for the value of this kind of study it must not of course be forgotten that it has its limitations. Its emphasis on the nature of the support for the different campaigns of 'first-wave' feminism leaves little time for the details of the campaigns themselves, and these details must be sought elsewhere (Banks 1981). Nor can there be any systematic account of the changes that have taken place in the lives of women during the period covered by the study, although these changes are nevertheless of very great significance if we are to understand developments within feminism itself (Lewis 1984). As a contribution to the understanding of 'first-wave' feminism therefore it takes its place alongside other studies and is in no sense intended to replace them. It is hoped, however, that as an alternative approach to feminist scholarship it will provide both new insights and new knowledge.

2   Who Were the Feminists?

It is often assumed that 'first-wave' feminism was essentially a middle-class movement, appealing predominantly to middle-class women and in fact an examination of the social origin of the female sample suggests that this assumption is largely if not wholly true. For the purpose of measuring social origin the sample was divided into four groups, according to father's occupation. This was made necessary because in the great majority of cases the mothers themselves had not worked either before marriage or indeed afterwards. Nor was there, in most cases, information on the social origin of the mothers themselves to provide an alternative system of classification. In most cases, however, the father's own occupation was given, and in sufficient detail to provide a four-fold classification, which covered landowners, who have been labelled gentry, professional men, business men, and working class. There was also a small group of women who could not be classified. This information is set out in Table 1, by cohort, in order to indicate change over time. Both the actual numbers and percentages within each cohort as well as for the total sample are provided. In this and subsequent tables percentages have been rounded off to the nearest whole number. This means that in some tables the percentages do not add up to 100.

It should be recalled that this sample represents the best-known of the feminists, and that many women in relatively humble positions in the movement have not been included. As a sample of activists however, it does represent the

10

Table 1: Social origin of female sample by cohort

	Gentry		Professional		Business		Working class		Not known		Total
	No.	%	No.	%	No.	%	No.	%	No.	%	No.
Cohort I	3	12	10	38	9	35	3	12	1	4	26
Cohort II	4	19	9	43	5	24	2	9	1	5	21
Cohort III	3	12	8	32	8	32	5	20	1	4	25
Cohort IV	0	0	9	35	8	31	6	23	3	12	26
Total	10	(10%)	36	(37%)	30	(31%)	16	(16%)	6	(6%)	98

leadership of 'first-wave' feminism and goes a long way to reinforce the impression that in its leadership at least it was a middle-class movement. A closer look at the table reveals, however, that this is true only with certain reservations. The land-owning group or 'gentry' is, for its size in the general population, well-represented, and the working class, if certainly under-represented, is by no means absent and in both cohort III and cohort IV begins to approach a quarter of the cohort. The professional category is the best represented but the business category does not fall far behind, and certainly these two groups taken together have dominated 'first-wave' feminism for most of its history. This should not, however, lead us to ignore the appeal of feminism to women from the gentry on the one hand, and working-class women on the other.

An alternative way of measuring the social class of the women in the sample is by means of their own occupation. This was made difficult by the fact that as many as 45 of the 98 women were not in any real sense of the term gainfully employed, although some of these published fairly extensively and even built up a professional reputation for themselves, like Adelaide Procter, who had a considerable reputation as a poet (Maison 1965) or Lady Emilia Dilke who was a distinguished art historian (Askwith 1969). If we look at those women, almost half of the sample, who were gainfully employed for at least some time during their lives, it is clear that it was almost entirely in the kind of semi-professional work open to middle-class women during this period. As many as 20, for example, were teachers of one kind or another, and a further nine were full-time journalists or professional writers, like Olive Schreiner, Evelyn Sharp or Cicely Hamilton. A small number had made their way, or indeed fought their way, into the predominantly masculine professions, three being doctors and one, Ethel Smyth, a well-known composer (St. John 1959). If we turn from this kind of employment to manual work we find only nine women, all from working-class backgrounds, falling into this category, so that the sample is in fact more middle-class in terms of its own occupation than in terms of its social origin. This is because the working-class sample contained a high proportion of women who, successful at school, subsequently trained as pupil-teachers.

The proportion of women who had been gainfully employed rose throughout the period of the study, reflecting changes over time in the pattern of employment of women in the middle classes (Lewis 1984) as well as the rising number of working-class women in the sample who would normally expect to work at least in the years before marriage. By cohort IV indeed, only three of the 26 women in the cohort had not been employed at any time in their lives. The occupations followed were more varied too, although teachers were still the largest group. Perhaps most striking is the extent to which this group became professional politicians, as many as five eventually entering the House of Commons, two of them, Margaret Bondfield and Ellen Wilkinson, from working-class backgrounds. A number of women in both cohorts III and IV also moved from their original occupation into paid employment within the women's movement, since both the Women's Social and Political Union and the National Union of Women's Suffrage Societies employed paid organisers in order to secure the services of working-class women. A number of these women, like Annie Kenney for example (Kenney 1924), or Ada Nield Chew (Chew 1982), had been manual workers, but others had been teachers, like Emily Davison (Colmore 1913).

In spite of this evidence of social mobility amongst working-class women in the sample, either through educational achievement or through politics, it was decided to keep social origin rather than own occupation as the measure of social class background. By this means it was possible to include almost all the women in the classification, which the use of their own occupation would not have done, and at the same time it preserved the experience of a working-class childhood.

If, however, the women's own occupation was rejected as a system of classification it was possible to differentiate within the sample in terms of education background. Although information on secondary education was almost always inadequate, details of higher education were available for the whole sample, and this information is given in Table 2, for each cohort, and for the total sample.

Table 2: Educational background of the female sample, by cohort

	Some higher education		No higher education		Total
	No.	%	No.	%	No.
Cohort I	3	12	23	88	26
Cohort II	6	29	15	71	21
Cohort III	9	36	16	64	25
Cohort IV	16	62	10	38	26
Total	34	35	64	65	98

The change over time reflects very clearly improvements in the education available to middle-class girls during the last decades of the nineteenth century. Higher education was virtually unavailable to the women in the first and indeed even in the second cohort, all of whom were born before 1847 and so were already young adults before higher education on any scale was opened to women. By cohort IV however, the majority of women in the sample were college educated, reflecting not simply a change in educational provision, although that was part of it, but also the attractions of feminism to the girl who had been to college, as well as college to the girl who was already a feminist. Educational level, as might be expected, was related closely to social origin. Only one (6%) of the 16 women of working-class origin had been to college compared with 45% of the professional and 36% of the business category. This renders even more remarkable the high level of college education in cohort IV, since almost a quarter of the women in that cohort are of working-class origin. Indeed, of the middle-class women in that cohort all but two had been to college or university. It is entirely fair, therefore, to argue that, as far as this sample is concerned, active feminists were not only predominantly middle-class, they were also, even for their class and period, unusually well educated.

The next stage in the analysis was an examination of the religious affiliation of the sample. This was by no means a straightforward exercise as the information necessary for the purpose was often not available, and indeed this is one of the areas in which the data for the sample is distressingly incomplete. Finally, the simple expedient was adopted in which known freethinkers or agnostics formed one category, those with some positive religious affiliation, of whatever kind, formed a second category, and those without any known religious affiliation formed a residual category. Some, and possibly many, in this group were freethinkers or at best indifferent to religion, which played no part in their lives, but it was considered safer to leave them in a category of their own. Another problem of classification occurred in those cases, and there were a number, in which there had been a distinct change of attitude over time. A very good example of this is Annie Besant, who moved from a strong religious affiliation to free thought and then, in middle age, to Theosophy (Nethercot 1961). Eventually it was decided to classify in terms of the religious affiliation during the period of active feminism. With this principle in mind, Annie Besant has been classified as a freethinker since, after her conversion to Theosophy, her feminist involvement declined very considerably.

Perhaps the most significant aspect of this table is the very high proportion of freethinkers especially in the early cohorts. Later the proportion of freethinkers declines but is more than made up for by the growth in the proportion of those with no known religious affiliation. If, however, religious scepticism and free thought represent an important tradition within feminism, it is by no means the only one. If those with a positive religious affiliation are, in the sample as a whole, in a minority (40%), it is a substantial not a small one which, in cohort I, is actually a majority and

Table 3: Religious affiliation of female sample, by cohort

	Freethinker		Positive religious affiliation		No known affiliation		Total
	No.	%	No.	%	No.	%	No.
Cohort I	9	35	15	58	2	8	26
Cohort II	9	43	8	38	4	19	21
Cohort III	6	24	7	28	12	48	25
Cohort IV	7	27	9	35	10	38	26
Total	31	32	39	40	28	29	98

which, although there is a decline over time, still includes 35% of cohort IV. In spite, therefore, of an association between secularism and feminism which led some women to define the Church as the chief agency in women's suppression (Taylor 1983) there were others, like Josephine Butler for example, who grounded their feminism in their religion (Boyd 1982).

An attempt was made to examine in more detail the religious affiliation of the women in the sample by listing, wherever this was known, the particular sect or denomination to which the woman in question belonged, but this revealed little in the way of a pattern, and the chief impression was of the wide variety of religious beliefs that appeared to be compatible with feminism. In the first generation of feminists, but only in this generation, both Quakers and Unitarians were prominent, but nonconformity as such was not important, and one of the most unexpected findings was the high proportion of feminists with an Anglican background. The chief distinguishing feature was not so much the sect or denomination itself, as the frequency with which the family background was described as infused with evangelical principles and evangelical piety.

There is a very clear relationship between social class origin and religious affiliation in so far as gentry are the most likely to have a positive religious affiliation (80%) and the working class the least (19%). The middle class are in an intermediate position with the business group less religiously oriented than the professional group. It is the

Table 4: Religious affiliation of female sample, by social origin

	Freethinker		Positive religious affiliation		No known religious affiliation		Total
	No.	%	No.	%	No.	%	No.
Gentry	2	20	8	80	0	0	0
Professional	10	28	16	44	10	28	36
Business	11	37	10	33	9	30	30
Working-class	5	31	3	19	8	50	16
Not known	3	50	2	33	1	17	6
Total	31	32	39	40	28	29	98

business group, too, who are most likely to be freethinkers (37%). The working-class group also contains a high proportion of freethinkers (31%), but it is also the group with the largest percentage (50%) of those with no known religious affiliation at all.

It is the upper and middle classes, therefore, who appear to be the main sources of the evangelical tradition within feminism. The working-class feminists are largely outside this tradition, although they share with the middle classes in the alternative tradition of religious scepticism and free thought. If, however, these two traditions are clearly present, it has still to be demonstrated that they had any influence on feminism itself, and this is an issue which will be explored in subsequent chapters.

Table 5: Political affiliation of female sample, by cohort

	Conservative		Liberal		Socialist		None or not known		Total
	No.	%	No.	%	No.	%	No.	%	No.
Cohort I	3	12	12	46	4	15	7	27	26
Cohort II	4	19	4	19	7	33	6	29	21
Cohort III	2	8	0	0	19	76	4	16	25
Cohort IV	1	4	0	0	15	58	10	38	26
Total	10	10	16	16	45	46	27	28	98

Although Table 5 speaks for itself to some extent, a few lines of explanation on the method and classification are necessary. There were some important changes of political affiliation and these have been dealt with as in the case of religious affiliation by ignoring those changes which occurred after any feminist involvement was at an end. Changes which occurred during the period of feminist involvement were more difficult to handle but in general the classification was chosen which seemed to represent the major political orientation over the period as a whole. Where there was no evidence of support for any particular political position, the category none or not known has been used. Where there was evidence of support or approval for one of the traditional nineteenth-century parties, this has been recorded as either Conservative or Liberal. The category 'Socialist' is more difficult to deal with since it represents an ideology rather than a political party as such. The category, therefore, includes those who were members of socialist groups like the Social Democratic Federation, the Fabians and the Independent Labour Party as well as the Labour Party itself. It also indicates all those who were Owenite socialists.

The most striking feature of the table is the way in which socialism dominates the two later cohorts. In cohort I the Liberals are the largest group, representing, at 46%, almost half the cohort, but the decline in support for the Liberals is rapid, and by Cohort III is altogether gone, its place taken by an extraordinary leap in the support for socialism, which now covers 76% of the cohort. Support for socialism has indeed always been a feature of feminism, and in each cohort it is higher than support for the Conservative party, but in cohort I it is the Owenite version of socialism which provides the link between socialism and feminism.

Owenite socialism, however, did not survive the 1840s and the rise in socialist support shown very dramatically in Table 5 had nothing at all to do with Owenism. Even feminists in cohort II, born as they were in the 1830s and 1840s, were too young to have been caught up in the Owenite movement and they turned to socialism largely in the 1880s and 1890s under the inspiration of the 'new' socialism which emerged in that period. A very good example is Annie

Besant who during the 1880s joined the Marxist inspired Social Democratic Federation and in 1888 organised the now famous 'match girl' strike (Nethercot 1961). She was in the vanguard of the movement towards socialism but during the 1890s many other feminists followed suit, like Emmeline Pankhurst who, with her husband Richard, joined the Independent Labour Party in 1894 (Mitchell 1967). By 1900 the majority of young women coming into feminism appear also to have been socialist in politics, which at this time appears to have had even closer ties to feminism than Liberalism during the nineteenth century. This situation was not to last, and cohort IV shows a looser relationship, although still a very strong one. Nor did Liberalism retain its position, and feminists who stood aloof from socialism tended, like Eleanor Rathbone, to define themselves politically as Independent (Stocks 1949).

Table 6: Political affiliation of female sample, by social origin

	Conservative		Liberal		Socialist		None or not known		Total
	No.	%	No.	%	No.	%	No.	%	No.
Gentry	4	40	3	30	1	10	2	20	10
Professional	1	3	6	17	16	44	13	36	36
Business	5	17	7	23	12	40	6	20	30
Working-class	0	0	0	0	13	81	3	19	16
Not known	0	0	0	0	3	50	3	50	3
Total	10	10	16	16	45	46	27	28	98

Clearly there is an association between social origin and political affiliation. Conservatism appealed to the gentry who had little interest in socialism. The working classes on the other hand were almost overwhelmingly socialist in their political affiliation. Nevertheless it is not possible to explain the swing to socialism in cohort III in terms of the increase in the number of working-class feminists at that time, even though such an increase, as Table 1 indicates, did in fact occur. A glance at the number of middle-class women who were socialists reveals the extent to which socialism was attractive to middle-class as well as to working-class women.

Indeed, of the 45 socialists in the sample, only 13 had a working-class social origin, compared with 29 from the upper and middle classes. Certainly the influx of working-class women into feminism played a part in bringing feminism and socialism together, but it does not seem to have played the major role. It may be argued that as feminism became more socialist in its outlook it was more attractive to working-class women, but the move towards socialism from within feminism seems to have been initiated largely by middle-class women.

Table 7: Political affiliation of female sample, by religious affiliation

	Freethinker		Positive religious affiliation		No known affiliation		Total
	No.	%	No.	%	No.	%	No.
Conservative	1	10	6	60	3	30	10
Liberal	8	50	8	50	0	0	16
Socialist	18	40	11	24	16	36	45
None or not known	4	15	14	52	9	33	27
Total	31		39		28		98

As Table 7 shows, the lowest level of religious affiliation was amongst socialist women (24%) and is undoubtedly a reflection, in part at least, of the proportion of the socialists in the sample who were of working-class origin. Indeed, of the eleven socialists who had a positive religious affiliation, ten were from the upper or middle classes.

At the same time, as many as twelve of the middle-class socialists were freethinkers. The socialist women, therefore, whether working-class or middle-class, were the least likely to be influenced by a religious motivation. The Conservatives present the opposite tendency with only one of the ten a freethinker, and as many as six with a positive religious affiliation. The Liberals are intermediate between the two, exactly half falling into each category. It is interesting to notice, however, that of the eight Liberals with a positive religious affiliation, two were Quakers and two were Unitarians. In general, therefore, although the picture is somewhat complex, it can be argued that in general terms the more radical the political position, the more radical, or at least the more sceptical, the position with respect to religious affiliation.

Although party politics is perhaps the most obvious way of classifying political affiliation, it can also be expressed in support for particular causes which are closer to pressure groups than to political parties. Indeed, the association between feminism and certain nineteenth-century pressure groups is already well known. In order to establish the degree of support for such pressure groups within this sample of feminists, any such involvement was noted wherever the information was available.

The most significant of these particular causes was the anti-slavery movement, which involved seven women (27%) in cohort I at a time when the movement was at its height in Britain, and a further two in cohort III by which time the movement was in decline. The incident in 1840 when women delegates from the United States were not allowed to take their seats at the London World Anti-Slavery Conference acted as a spur to several women prominent in the anti-slavery movement in Britain, of whom Anne Knight is perhaps the best known. From this time forward she was an ardent advocate of women's suffrage, bombarding her friends with leaflets and lecturing on women's rights at both peace and temperance meetings (Tyrrell 1980, Taylor 1983). A number of feminists of this period, including Barbara Bodichon and Harriet Martineau, also drew attention to the very direct affinity between the position of women and the position of slaves (Reed 1972, Pichanick 1980).

Another movement frequently associated with feminism was the Anti-Corn Law League. This was less significant than the anti-slavery movement, involving only five women altogether, four in cohort I, and one in cohort II. Equally important was the cause of Italian unity which also involved five women in the sample, four in cohort II and one in cohort I. If we take these three movements together we find that they involve no less than 40% of the women in the first two cohorts, a clear indication of the extent to which these early feminists were associated with other movements for social reform.

These three causes had, however, achieved their objectives well before the end of the nineteenth century, and it is no surprise to find that women in cohorts III and IV were no longer involved in any of these issues. In any case, feminism itself was changing, its political affiliation moving from Liberalism to socialism, and this is reflected in the kind of issues which now gained feminist support. The most important of these was pacifism, which claimed the attention of ten women in cohort III and three women in cohort IV. Of these 13 women, moreover, only one was not a socialist, indicating that for these women pacifism was part of the same movement of ideas which led them from feminism to socialism.

The only other important issue which emerged from this analysis was temperance. The links between temperance and feminism were very strong in the United States, but in Britain the two movements tended to go their separate ways, and this is reflected in the fact that only four women in the sample were active in the temperance cause. Of these, two were in cohort I, one in cohort III and one in cohort IV. This is the only issue, of those considered, which stretches across the whole period of 'first-wave' feminism.

If we turn now to answer the question with which this chapter began, the question of who the feminists were, the answer appears to be a somewhat complex one. They emerge, it is true, as chiefly middle-class in social origin but, by the final cohort at least, nearly a quarter were from a working-class background. Working-class feminism, therefore, is by no means an insignificant aspect of 'first-wave' feminism as Liddington and Norris have clearly shown in their study of women textile workers (Liddington and Norris 1978) and the part they played within the women's movement will need to be examined in detail in subsequent chapters. Already, however, from the data presented in this chapter it is evident that they were different as a group from middle- and upper-class feminists, since they were less likely to have a positive religious affiliation and considerably more likely to be socialist in their political affiliation. They were also considerably less likely to have been to college and university.

The religious affiliation of the feminists ranged from atheists and freethinkers to Anglicans and, in three cases, all converts, Roman Catholics. Free thought was, however, a very significant element, especially in the first two cohorts, and in cohort II it was the largest category of all. In the later cohorts both free thought and religious belief declined, to be replaced by the indifference to religion characteristic of a largely secularised society. Positive religious affiliation was not, however, randomly distributed in the sample. It was associated with social origin, where it was most frequent amongst the gentry, and it was also associated with Conservatism in politics. The extent to which it may be defined as a distinct tradition within feminism, representing a different kind of feminist involvement and a different feminist ideology has, however, still to be determined.

The most interesting and indeed the most unexpected finding in this chapter relates to political affiliation. Although the first generation of feminists was predominantly Liberal in politics, this association between Liberalism and feminism drops with remarkable rapidity to be replaced by socialism, which in cohort III is quite clearly the dominating factor in the sample. Moreover, although the gentry remain outside this movement towards socialism, it has clearly influenced both the professional and to a lesser extent the business classes. Working-class feminists are almost all socialist in their political affiliation. For reasons which are by no means clear the association between feminism and socialism declines in cohort IV, although at 58% it is still the political affiliation of more than half the sample. Nevertheless, in the sample as a whole socialists are the largest group, making up 46% of the total and considerably overshadowing the Liberals who are important only in the very early days of the women's movement.

The other feature of this examination of the political affiliation of the female sample is the absence of any close tie between feminism and Conservatism at least in its expression as a political movement. Throughout its history 'first-wave' feminism tended to be associated with the party of political and social reform and in many respects, as will be shown later, this is manifested in the actual programme of the women's movement. Indeed one of the arguments to be made in subsequent chapters is that feminism was not isolated from either social or political history, but was part and parcel of a much wider movement not only for social change but for what can only be called social reformation.

An important aspect of the change in affiliation from Liberalism to socialism, to which further attention will need to be paid, is the period at which it occurred. In cohort I, in spite of the very active presence of the Owenites, the socialists represent only 15% of the group, compared with 46% who were Liberal in their political affiliation. By cohort II, however, the socialists represent 33% of the group and the Liberals 19%. Moreover, as was indicated earlier, this increase in the number of socialist feminists occurred at the same time as the decline in Owenite socialism and was associated in fact with new developments in socialism which began during the 1880s and which led eventually to the foundation of the modern Labour movement. During the 1880s and 1890s however, the 'new socialism' found its political expression mainly in groups like the Social Democratic Federation, the Socialist League, the Fabians, and the Independent Labour Party. Although the Social Democratic Federation tended to be anti-feminist, this was not true of the rest, and the Independent Labour Party in particular employed several feminists as speakers and organisers, a fact which was to have significant consequences for the recruitment of feminists to socialism and socialists to feminism (Rowbotham 1973, Rowbotham and Weeks 1977).

The decline of Liberal feminism therefore occurred at a time when the Liberal party was still the main alternative government and before the rise of the Labour Party as an electoral challenge to either of the main parties. Indeed, there is evidence in this study that the rise of the Labour Party was associated with the decline not only of socialism within feminism but even, for reasons which will be discussed later, with the decline of feminism itself. Nevertheless, we may with reason describe the Liberal ascendancy as lasting until the 1880s, reaching its peak between the decline of Owenite feminism during the 1840s and the rise of the 'new' socialism in the late 1880s. The significance of this change for feminism will be the main subject matter of several subsequent chapters.

In the meantime, however, Chapter 3 turns away from the social and political context of the women's movement and describes the personal relationships these feminists experienced with those closest to them. These experiences may be seen as one source of feminism and will be explored in this context. At the same time feminism may itself react on these experiences determining, for example, a woman's response to both sex and marriage, and this too will be examined in so far as the evidence allows. In this way an extra and more personal dimension will be added to the picture already drawn of the social and political background of the women in the sample.

3 Intimate Relationships

In spite of the attention given to the childhood experiences of feminists like Harriet Martineau, Florence Nightingale and Olive Schreiner we have very little systematic knowledge of the relationship between feminists and their parents which might lead us to some general conclusions about the effect of childhood experiences on the development of feminist attitudes in later life. Biographers have given us interesting insights in individual cases (Woodham Smith 1951), but no one has attempted an analysis which throws light on the genesis of feminism in general rather than particular terms. For this reason it was judged important to include this dimension in the present analysis, and for this purpose an attempt was made to classify the nature of parent/child relationships for each of the women in the sample in order to discover the existence of any pattern which might help in understanding the process which turned them into feminists. Unfortunately, the detailed information necessary for this kind of analysis was frequently unavailable so that the analysis which follows is necessarily incomplete. Nevertheless, it is hoped that the findings will prove useful even so, bearing in mind the lack of previous analysis in this field and the problems which necessarily arise in the use of biographical and autobiographical material.

The first dimension to be examined was that of affection. Fathers and mothers separately were classified as close and warm or cold and distant to this particular child in the light of all the available information, and this analysis is provided in Table 8.

Table 8: Nature of relationship with parents of the female sample

	Affectionate		Cold		Absent		Not known		Total
	No.	%	No.	%	No.	%	No.	%	No.
Father	37	38	10	10	13	13	38	39	98
Mother	24	24	15	15	10	10	49	50	98

The absence of information is unfortunate but it is note-worthy that both fathers and mothers are much more likely to be described as affectionate than as cold and distant. Even more interesting is the fact that, in spite of the stereo-type of nineteenth-century mothers as loving and fathers as distant and even authoritarian, mothers are more likely to be described by biographers as cold than are fathers. It is difficult to interpret this finding when the group of 'cold' mothers was so small, and clearly there is no justification here for the conclusion that feminism in general was based on rejection by a cold or rejecting mother. On the other hand, in individual cases this rejection or perceived rejection may have played some part. It is difficult to read Olive Schreiner's life story, for example, without concluding that her difficult relationship with her mother was the key to understanding her own ambivalent attitude to marriage and motherhood (First and Scott 1980, Berkman 1979). Harriet Martineau's belief that she was rejected by her mother may well have played a part in her own, frequently expressed, sense of unworthiness as a woman and her drive for other kinds of achievement (Martineau 1877), and it is noteworthy that other women whose relationship with their mothers was unhappy, like Marie Stopes for example (Hall 1977) and Florrence Nightingale (Woodham Smith 1951) also show this same drive for achievement. If, therefore, we should be cautious about the extent of this kind of relationship and its significance for feminism in general, it may well be important as one route to the rejection of conventional attitudes to women.

Very few fathers have been classified as cold or unaffec-tionate, so that unloving fathers seem even less promising as a factor in the process of becoming a feminist than unloving mothers. Indeed because, customarily, Victorian fathers had little to do with small children, struggles with their father often only occurred when the years of childhood were over and the personality was fully developed. Frances Power Cobbe, for example, had a close and affectionate relationship with her mother and, although her father was a remote figure, she only came into conflict with him after her mother's death when she confessed to him her growing doubt about religion (Cobbe 1894). On the whole, however, the fathers in this sample are notable for their affectionate relationship with their daughters. Indeed, fathers were considerably more likely to be classed as affectionate than mothers, who fall more frequently into the category 'cold' but more frequently still into the category 'unknown'. Indeed one of the features of this study generally was how much less information biographers provide about mothers than about fathers.

A breakdown in terms both of the four cohorts and by social origin failed to reveal any pattern of differences. For example, although 12% of working-class fathers were classed as 'cold', so were 11% of professional fathers. On the whole, therefore, this particular classification did not seem helpful in understanding changes either over time or in terms of social class background and, if it has a value, it is mainly in underlining the complexity of the issue and the problems that face us in our search for understanding.

The second dimension of parent/child relationships to be examined was parental encouragement. Again, mothers and fathers were classified separately and were defined as encouraging if, in general terms, they supported the desire of their daughters to be independent or in some other way different or unconventional. Discouraging parents were those who tried to prevent their daughters from breaking out of the traditional female role.

Table 9: Level of parental encouragement for female sample

	Encourage-ment		Discourage-ment		Neutral		Absent		Not known		Total
	No.	%	No.	%	No.	%	No.	%	No.	%	No.
Fathers	32	33	9	9	19	19	13	13	25	25	98
Mothers	21	21	13	13	18	18	10	10	36	37	98

The level of encouragement shown in Table 9 is high, especially for fathers, and the level of discouragement low, especially when it is remembered that this is a sample of women whose behaviour was generally unconventional. Once again the number in the unknown category is high, and some parents were classed as neutral when they appear to have played a predominantly neutral role. Parents classified as encouraging include all those who took a special interest in the education of their daughters at a time when such an interest was rare, sometimes, in the case of fathers particularly, by taking part in it themselves. Margaret Nevinson's father, himself a clergyman, taught his daughter Latin and Greek at a time when such studies were considered unsuitable for a girl (Nevinson 1926). Other parents, and again this was frequently the father rather than the mother, took a particular pride in the literary or professional achievements of their daughter and encouraged her to break through into what had formerly been a man's world. Perhaps the best example of this attitude is provided by the father of Elizabeth Garrett Anderson. His initial shock on learning that she wanted to train as a doctor soon gave way to the most vigorous support and encouragement (Manton 1965).

Mothers were less likely to be encouraging than fathers and more likely to be discouraging, and this was undoubtedly because they were on the whole more likely to be conventional in their attitudes to women. Elizabeth Garrett Anderson's mother, for example, begged her with tears and entreaties not to train as a doctor (Manton 1965), and the mother of Florence Nightingale was equally appalled at her daughter's decision to train as a nurse (Woodham Smith 1951). By the end of the century the situation was beginning to change but Evelyn Sharp's mother, for example, still believed that an unmarried daughter's place was at home (Sharp 1933). Similarly, Margaret Nevinson's mother believed that any marriage was better than no marriage at all, and was furious when Margaret turned down a proposal from an elderly and unattractive neighbour (Nevinson 1926).

Interestingly, in many such cases, support for the daughter was provided by the father and it was in fact rare to find an example of discouragement from both parents. Indeed there are only three such examples, one of which was Florence Nightingale, and it is not without significance that her mother was even more disapproving of her than her father, to whom she was in many respects very close (Woodham Smith 1951). Another example is Helena Swanwick whose desire to go to Girton College in 1882 was opposed by both her parents, and only the intervention of a godmother made it possible for her to achieve her ambition (Swanwick 1935).

Discouraging fathers were rarer than discouraging mothers, although their attitude too was based mainly on conventional attitudes to women. The rarity of such fathers in the sample, combined with the evidence from the earlier table that on the whole the women in the study had a good relationship with their father, suggests the possibility that, for many women at least, their attempts to lead independent and even unconventional lives were actually supported and even encouraged by their fathers, who were themselves men of somewhat unconventional views with respect to women. Discouraging fathers on the other hand may well have had the power not only to discourage their daughters' desire to live their own lives but actually to thwart it. Indeed the evidence from the nine examples in the study suggests that discouraging fathers had more power over their daughters than discouraging mothers simply because they had power over their wives too as well as the family purse-strings. With the support of her enthusiastic father Elizabeth Garrett Anderson could ignore the plaints of her mother, but it was more difficult for Ethel Smyth to overcome the opposition of her autocratic father when she faced him with her ambition to study music. Her final victory was achieved only when she faced him with a will as strong as his own (Smyth 1923). Constance Lytton, on the other hand, abandoned her own ambition to study music and lived at home as a dutiful daughter until she was well into middle age (Lytton 1914). Far from feminism being a reaction against an autocratic father, therefore, it seems more likely to be the response to a father whose own unconventionality of views encouraged a similar unconventionality in his daughter.

If, on the other hand, mothers were less encouraging than

fathers, encouraging mothers were by no means absent from the sample. Moreover, such mothers were quite frequently feminists themselves. Emmeline Pankhurst, for example, was taken to suffrage meetings by her mother when she was quite a young child and she in her turn introduced her daughters to the movement (Mitchell 1967). Another mother who successfully passed her feminism to her daughter was Charlotte Carmichael, the mother of Marie Stopes (Hall 1977). If, therefore, unconventional fathers played their part, so too did unconventional mothers, and for daughters brought up in this kind of family, like Emmeline and Sylvia Pankhurst for example, their support for feminism was in no way a rebellion against their parents. The significance of this finding for the process of becoming a feminist will be discussed in a later chapter.

An attempt to relate parental encouragement to social origin failed to achieve any meaningful pattern of answers. Fathers' encouragement was highest in the professional group (47%) but for mothers it was highest amongst the gentry (40%). In the working-class group, the proportion in the unknown category was at its highest, and so was the proportion in the neutral group. Consequently, almost no working-class parents are classified as either discouraging or encouraging. It is not clear however whether this reflects our lack of knowledge of the childhood experiences of the working-class sample or a difference in working-class experience.

The pattern of relationship between affection and encouragement is also a complex one. Twelve mothers were both affectionate and encouraging, but ten were neutral and two were discouraging. These were affectionate but conventional women who disapproved of their daughters' attempt at independence. On the other hand, cold mothers were not necessarily discouraging. The mother of Marie Stopes, for example, a reserved woman who was unable to maintain a loving relationship with either her husband or children, encouraged her daughter in her academic ambitions and was indeed ambitious for her (Hall 1977). Fathers classed as affectionate were also mainly encouraging although some were classified as neutral. Cold fathers were not necessarily discouraging however, for some were neutral and one, the father of Emmeline Pethick-Lawrence, was a distant and rather frightening figure in her childhood but later on gave her support and encouragement (Pethick-Lawrence 1938).

Although attention so far has been focused on parent/child relationships, siblings could also be important. Indeed in some respects brothers, even younger brothers, could take on many of the characteristics of a father, especially after the father's death. One of the best known examples of such a brother is James Martineau, Harriet's younger brother. In later life they quarrelled bitterly, but as children and adolescents they studied together and it was at his suggestion that she turned to writing, at first simply to occupy her time while he was away at college, but later as a way to earn a living. His encouragement, and that of an older brother, was particularly important to her because of the lack of encouragement from her parents and especially her mother (Pichanick 1980). Another brother who played a similar role was Arthur Clough the poet, whose sister Anne Jemima Clough became the first Principal of Newnham. Given an inferior education because she was a girl, it was Arthur who directed her reading and later her ambitions, and there is no doubt that he was the most important person in her life (Clough 1903). Another supportive brother was Lord Lytton, the brother of Lady Constance Lytton. Motivated by his sympathy and affection for his sister, he not only championed her within the family during her prison experiences but became the acknowledged leader of the pro-suffrage faction in the House of Lords (Lytton 1914). The relationship between Emily Davies and her brother John Llewellyn Davies was also important both for her and for the women's movement generally. A clergyman influenced by Christian socialism, he became, through his sister, involved with women's higher education and particularly women's entry into higher education (Manton 1965). His daughter, Margaret Llewellyn Davies, was also a feminist who, through her work for the Co-operative Women's Guild, devoted her life to the cause of working-class women (Gaffin and Thoms 1983).

If, however, brothers could sometimes take on the role of a supportive father, they were also significant as a source of resentment and jealousy, drawing attention to the limitations imposed on women by conventional attitudes. This was most likely to happen when a brother went away to school or college and his sister was left behind, although it could also occur when a brother was allowed an independent career and his sister was not. The fact that a brother and sister had been loving companions as children may well have increased the feelings of loss and deprivation, especially when they had actually studied together, and the knowledge that they had as much intellectual ability as their brothers fuelled the feminism of a number of women in the sample, especially in the first two cohorts, who grew up at a time when higher education was altogether closed to women. Emily Davies, for example, built her life-long commitment to women's education on her own longing to go to Cambridge as her brother had done (Stephen 1927). Elizabeth Wolstenholme Elmy too, resented bitterly the fact that she was given a purely domestic education while her brother went to Cambridge (Ethelmer 1896).

Relationships with sisters were also significant although in different ways. When they inspired jealousy it was not because they represented a freer and more independent way of life but because they had a sweetness of disposition which earned them the affection and respect not only of their parents but of others around them. Mary Carpenter, for example, was convinced as a child, and indeed well into adult life, that she was unloved and unlovable, and envied her young sister her amiable nature (Carpenter 1879). The childhood of Sophia Jex-Blake was also overshadowed by an older sister who was docile and well behaved in contrast to Sophia's naughtiness (Todd 1918), and Harriet Martineau was jealous of an obedient younger sister (Pichanick 1980). These women found it difficult even as children to fit into the conventional stereotype of compliant girlhood without which they believed they could not achieve the love they sought. Women like this might easily come to doubt their own femininity and to seek the recognition they craved in the world of intellectual or political achievement.

By no means all sisterly relationships fall into this category and it would be wrong to exaggerate its importance. Other sisters were both friends and colleagues who worked together in the women's movement, like the two Shirreff sisters, Emily Shirreff and her sister Maria Grey. Pioneers in the early stages of the movement for women's education, they published a number of books jointly both before and after Maria's marriage (Ellsworth 1979). Also prominent in feminist history are the Garrett sisters. Louise, the eldest, had been drawn into radical and feminist circles during the 1850s after she married and moved to London, and she was able to give a good deal of support and encouragement to her sister Elizabeth, later Elizabeth Garrett Anderson, when she herself moved to London to train as a doctor. It was Louise too who took her young sister Millicent, not yet eighteen, to hear one of John Stuart Mill's elective addresses, and it was on a visit to Louise not long afterwards that Millicent met her future husband Henry Fawcett. Both were to become active in the suffrage movement, and on his death Millicent Fawcett became the leader of the constitutional suffrage movement (Manton 1965).

In trying, therefore, to understand the part played by family relationships in the making of a feminist, it is obvious that no simple explanation will suffice. The women in the sample had very different kinds of relationships with both their parents and their siblings, and there is little common ground upon which to work. The position is further complicated by the lack of information, especially for mothers, which naturally casts some doubt on the findings themselves. What does emerge, however, is the extent to which fathers, and to a lesser degree brothers, were themselves, if not actually feminists, unconventional in their views on the role of women. Indeed although some mothers were, exceptionally, feminists, most of the mothers, so far as our information goes, were more conventional than the fathers. The implications of this finding are highly important and will be explored in more detail in subsequent chapters. It does suggest, however, that family background may be more significant for its ideological than for its psychological influences.

The other intimate relationship to be analysed in this chapter is marriage. The most obvious distinction in this connection is between those who were married and those who were not, but the actual experience of marriage and of motherhood is also, perhaps, likely to be even more significant. Account must also be taken of relationships outside marriage involving either sex or love or both between men and women or, whether the relationship was explicitly lesbian or not, between women. In contrast to the lack of biographical detail on childhood, most of this information is readily available, so that the tables that follow are for the first time in this chapter virtually complete and, on the whole, reliably accurate.

The popular stereotype of 'first-wave' feminists held during the late nineteenth century frequently depicted them as women who had failed to find a husband and had turned to the women's movement in a spirit of bitterness and despair. As Table 10 shows, this stereotype is misleading. Even when the marital status of women is confined to their period of activity in the women's movement, only 46% were unmarried, and no more than 11% were widowed or separated.

Table 10: Marital status of female sample during all or part of their feminist involvement, by cohort

	Married		Unmarried		Widowed or Separated		Total
	No.	%	No.	%	No.	%	No.
Cohort I	6	23	14	54	6	23	26
Cohort II	13	62	6	29	2	10	21
Cohort III	13	52	10	40	2	8	25
Cohort IV	10	38	15	58	1	4	26
Total	42	43	45	46	11	11	98

Although overall the proportion of married and unmarried women is roughly equal, the variation between cohorts is considerable. Nor does it follow any simple pattern. Single women (54%) are in the majority in cohort I, and when we add to this the 23% of women who were separated or widowed, and in this respect single, the proportion of married women falls to only 23%. The first generation of feminists, therefore, were drawn predominantly from women who were married or whose marriage had ended. To this extent it represented the popular stereotype. By cohort II, however, the picture had changed dramatically. Only 29% of the cohort were unmarried, and as many as 62% were married women living with their husbands. This second generation of feminists, born between 1828 and 1848, who were really the founders of feminism as an organised movement, were therefore largely married women. After cohort II the picture changes again. The proportion of married women gradually falls, and the proportion of unmarried women rises, and cohort IV actually has, at 58%, more unmarried women than cohort I. Indeed the difference between cohort I and cohort IV is largely in the much smaller proportion of widowed or separated women in cohort IV.

Clearly, therefore, single women did have a particularly important part to play in the women's movement, although it could never at any time be described as a movement of spinsters. Nor when we look more closely at the single women in the sample do we find very much resemblance to the frustrated spinsters of popular imagination. Indeed for a large number spinsterhood was entirely a matter of choice. Florence Nightingale is perhaps the best known example of a woman who put her concept of her mission before marriage, rejecting several proposals including one from a man she genuinely loved (Woodham Smith 1951). The eminent headmistress Dorothea Beale also had several marriage proposals, the last when she was well into middle age. She believed firmly, however, that women like herself found a greater fulfilment in work than in marriage (Kamm 1958). There was also a number of women who had no sexual interest in men, like Sophia Jex-Blake, whose passionate but unrequited love for Octavia Hill lasted all her life (Todd 1918). Others, like Frances Power Cobbe (Cobbe 1894) and Eleanor Rathbone (Stocks 1949) found life-long companionship and great happiness with another woman.

Not every woman who remained unmarried fell into this category. Both Mary Carpenter (Carpenter 1879) and Ann Jemima Clough (Clough 1903) dreamed of love and marriage and yearned, unrequitedly, for an ideal partner to share their lives. Frances Buss was forced, at great emotional cost to herself, to put aside the hope of marriage in order to educate her young brothers (Kamm 1958). Nevertheless amongst the women in the sample, including some who eventually married, there was a sense of anxiety about the marriage state which derived from the doctrine of the subordination of the wife enshrined not only in the law but in religion and custom. Writing in 1858, the unmarried Emily Shirreff warned women that 'acquiescence in the superiority of man as a general law does not imply acknowledgment of superiority in particular instances', and she argued that it was better to remain unmarried than to give themselves to a man unequal to them in intellect or worth of character (Shirreff 1858, p. 276). Barbara Bodichon's study of the law affecting married women filled her with a dread of marriage, which was only stilled when she met a liberal-minded Frenchman who was prepared to marry her on her terms (Burton 1949). Olive Schreiner was another woman who feared to lose her freedom in marriage and she did not in fact marry until middle age (First and Scott 1980).

It should perhaps be emphasised at this point that for almost all these women the rejection of marriage meant the acceptance of life-long chastity and the sacrifice of their hopes for children. Unconventional in many of their attitudes, they were in most cases completely conventional in their attitude to sex outside marriage. Women living apart from their husbands felt obliged to accept these rules so that Harriet Taylor, for example, felt constrained to maintain a platonic relationship with John Stuart Mill until the death of her husband freed them to marry (Hayek 1951, Rossi 1970). Single women in love with married men were constrained by the same sexual morality, even at great cost to themselves, as Maude Royden's moving account of her life-long relationship with the Reverend Hudson Shaw makes abundantly clear (Royden 1947).

Indeed in the sample as a whole only a very few women stepped outside these rigid rules of morality. Two, Emma Martin and Elizabeth Sharples contracted common-law marriages because they were not able to marry, but both of these moved outside conventional middle-class circles. Sylvia Pankhurst also entered into a common-law marriage, although for reasons of principle rather than necessity

(Mitchell 1967, Pankhurst 1979). Ethel Smyth also refused marriage on the same grounds although she was sufficiently conventional to refuse sex to her married lover until the death of his wife freed him from the relationship (St. John 1959). Stella Browne, one of the few women in the sample who openly condemned conventional morality, also appears to have lived an unconventional life and is indeed the only woman in the sample who is known to have had an abortion (Rowbotham 1977). Five women in the sample conceived before marriage, two of them from working-class backgrounds. Of the rest, one, Frances Wright, was influenced by Owenite socialism and an advocate of free love, although even she married once she knew she was pregnant (Lane 1972). Rather more adventurous was Elizabeth Wolstenholme who had intended to dispense with the marriage ceremony altogether as a protest against the marriage laws, but who was persuaded by her colleagues in the suffrage movement to abandon her principle to maintain the respectability of the movement (Pankhurst 1931). The general picture, therefore, is of women who, whatever their private feelings may have been, lived within the sexual conventions of their time.

In any consideration of the single women as a group however, it should be remembered that they are in fact a somewhat miscellaneous collection which runs from women who were in fact in love with a man, and even in a very few cases lived with him, to women who lived all their adult lives in complete harmony with another woman. Some women, although attracted to men, refused marriage on the grounds of principles, while others longed for an ideal partnership that never materialised. All of them, however, except the two single women involved in common-law marriages, necessarily stood outside the Victorian ideal of wife and mother, even if it was by their own desire, and it is from this group that we might expect to find the concern for the status of the spinster which was a significant feature of nineteenth-century feminism. Subsequent chapters will therefore examine in detail the part played by single women, as opposed to married women, in the development of 'first-wave' feminism.

Those women who were or had been married at the time

of their involvement in the women's movement were further
sub-divided into those with successful and those with unsuccessful marriages. Nine of the married women in the sample
were excluded for lack of data, but there was enough information on the rest to make an assessment even if there is
perhaps some preferences on the part of biographers for
happy marriages. Of these marriages 26 were successful,
and 18 unsuccessful. These 18 are all first marriages
however, and four of these women made a successful
marriage, one of these a common-law marriage, the second
time round. Indeed, only one woman, Marie Stopes, seems
to have made two unsuccessful marriages (Hall 1977). So
far as 'first-wave' feminism is concerned, therefore, it
appears to be associated more closely with happy than with
unhappy marriages. There were, however, sufficient unsuccessful marriages to make it possible to consider the effect
of an unhappy marriage on the making of a feminist.
Biographies of Caroline Norton, for example, make it abundantly clear that it was the experience of her disastrous
marriage to George Norton and what it taught her in
personal terms of the legal status of married women that
drove her to take action to change the law on the custody
of children and which led to the Infant Custody Act of 1839
(Holcombe 1983, Forster 1984). Similarly Annie Besant,
Anna Wheeler, Anna Jameson (Thomas 1967) and Emma
Martin were deeply influenced by the breakdown of their
marriage and its consequences so that, if it was not the only
reason for their later feminism, it was an influence of very
considerable importance. Yet in other cases an unhappy
marriage seems to have been irrelevant or even, in some
cases, a consequence of a wife's desire for independence.
The marriage of Lady Rhondda, for example, ended in
divorce but there is no evidence that either the marriage
breakdown or her relationship with her husband had any
effect on her feminism (Rhondda 1933). Both Frances
Wright and Olive Schreiner were already feminists when
they married, and both, but perhaps Frances Wright most
of all, found married life constraining, and both eventually
left their husbands (First and Scott 1980, Lane 1972). The
relationship is, therefore, a complex one and will be examined in more detail in subsequent chapters.

The juxtaposition between active feminists and marital happiness requires perhaps more explanation. At first it may perhaps seem that the happiness of the marriage is a consequence of the reticence of the biography and in some cases this may be true. For many, and perhaps even most of the women in this category, it is manifestly untrue, and the reason, in so far as a reason can be found, lies in the affinity of ideas between husband and wife and the extent to which the husband was prepared to give encouragement and support to his wife in her involvement in the women's movement itself. Nor was this in most cases simply a happy accident. Many women, especially those who already had some commitment to feminism before their marriage, searched deliberately for a husband who shared their views, and would not commit themselves to marriage without some assurance on this point, insisting for example on some such gesture as the omission of the word obey from the marriage service. This was perhaps the commonest gesture but some couples, like the Pethick-Lawrences and the Billington-Greigs, joined their names, and sometimes the wife retained her own name. When Alice Vickery married Charles Drysdale, for example, she was known as Alice Drysdale Vickery, and Florence Fenwick Miller retained her own name when she married Frederick Ford, adding only the prefix Mrs. None of these expedients seems very radical today but they must have seemed so at the time. Indeed there was an unsuccessful attempt to upset Florence Fenwick Miller's election to the London School Board on the grounds of the illegality of her name (Van Arsdel 1979).

In the sample as a whole there was in fact very little outright opposition to a wife's feminist activity even when it caused the husband considerable domestic activity, and with certain notable exceptions husbands were tolerant even when they were not exactly in approval. Indeed the evidence from this study suggests that marriages did not survive the active opposition of a husband to his wife's need for independence. Even more striking perhaps is the number of husbands who were active partners with their wives in the women's movement. As many as fourteen husbands come into this category, a number of whom were important enough to have been included in the sample of male feminists. Other men, like George Butler for example, gave such encouragement, support and active sympathy to their wives that they might equally well be described as partners (Butler 1892).

This sample of women has of course been chosen on the basis of their active participation in the women's movement, and for this reason the approval of their husbands has been of particular importance. Involvement in a feminist campaign meant the sacrifice of time which, even with several servants, usually implied some degree of sacrifice on the part of the husband too. Moreover, in many campaigns absences from home were lengthy, and in the militant suffrage campaign in particular might involve a prison sentence and the very real threat to health of a hunger strike and forcible feeding. Edith Rigby, for example, was away from home for long periods, sometimes in hiding, so that even her husband did not know where to find her. A suffrage supporter himself, Charles Rigby was proud of his wife's courage and not only accepted that her sacrifice was necessary but sprang readily to her defence when it was required (Hesketh 1966).

Domestic servants, if they could not take the place of an absent wife, must nevertheless have made life easier for middle-class women, and may help to explain why fewer working-class women took an active part, especially in the suffrage campaign. Hannah Mitchell has documented the problems facing the working-class wife who wanted a public life of her own. Although her husband shared her views and sympathised with her work, he was not prepared to take an active part in either housework or cooking, and she relied a good deal on friendly and helpful neighbours (Mitchell 1977b). This seems to have been typical of working-class husbands who, however sympathetic in principle to their wives' work outside the home, still left the domestic arrangements in their hands. Ada Chew, for example, used her own earnings as an organiser for the Women's Trade Union League to pay for someone to care for her daughters (Chew 1982).

Given the problems facing married women, therefore, it is not surprising to find that so many of the most active feminists were single women. This is not to suggest that such women had no domestic ties. A number of them were left with the responsibility of elderly parents, which tied them down, often, like Ann Jemima Clough, into early middle age (Clough 1903), and the expectation that single daughters, whether in the middle or the working classes, would remain at home with their mothers pressed upon single women throughout most, if not all, the period covered by this study. The contrast between single and married women should not, therefore, be pushed too far. Nevertheless single women on the whole probably had more freedom as well as more time at their disposal than married women, especially where they had to satisfy the needs not only of a husband but of children. Indeed, a family of young children may well have posed more problems than a husband especially when, as we have seen, the women in the study tended to have husbands who were tolerant if not actually supportive. It comes as no real surprise, therefore, to find that the women in the sample had small families for their period.

Table 11: Family size of married female sample, by cohort

	0	1	2	3	4	5	6	Not known	Total
Cohort I	4	0	2	3	1	1	1	0	12
Cohort II	3	4	2	2	3	0	1	0	15
Cohort III	4	4	4	0	0	2	1	0	15
Cohort IV	2	2	3	2	0	0	0	2	11
Total	13	10	11	7	4	3	3	2	53

For most of the period covered by the study family size in the middle classes was falling, and this is reflected in cohort IV which shows a decline in large families. If this is expected from general demographic trends however, the complete absence of really large families, even in the early cohorts, is not, and must reflect the extent to which women with really large families were tied to the demands of the nursery for the greater part of their active lives. Several women in the sample had been born into such families, including women from the later as well as the earlier cohorts. Frances Balfour in cohort III, for example, was the tenth of twelve children, and Emmeline Pethick-Lawrence in the same cohort the second of thirteen. Yet in this sample the largest number of children in any cohort was six, and only six women had more than four children. The other surprise is the very large proportion (25%) of married women who were childless.

Although some of the women in the sample deliberately restricted the size of their families, it is likely that the childlessness was involuntary and there is little evidence of the kind of rejection of motherhood that was felt by a number of women towards marriage. It is possible that some of the women who felt no inclination to marry had no desire for children either, but others, like Florence Nightingale for example, were all too painfully aware that their refusal to marry meant the sacrifice of any hope of children (Woodham Smith 1951). Moreover, many of the childless married women bitterly regretted their failure to have children, and this applied even to those who had feared marriage as a threat to their independence. Barbara Bodichon, for example, longed desperately but unavailingly for a child (Burton 1949), and Olive Schreiner, who lost her only child shortly after its birth, never really recovered from the shock and disappointment (First and Scott 1980). Only amongst working-class women does there seem to have been any appreciation of the costs of child-bearing to a woman, and it is in this group that we find the clearest evidence of a deliberate attempt to restrict the size of family. Ada Chew, for example, determined to have one child, and only one, and in this determination, although we do not know precisely how it was achieved, she was successful (Chew 1982). Hannah Mitchell too made the deliberate decision to restrict her family to one child (Mitchell 1977b), and Selina Cooper whose first child, conceived before marriage, died as an infant, had one further child only (Liddington 1984).

The significance of the low family size of this sample of feminists lies, therefore, less in what it tells us about the attitude to motherhood than in the opportunity it provided to these women to become active in the women's movement. This is most obvious in the case of working-class women, but even a middle-class woman would have found it difficult to combine an active involvement in feminism with the needs of a large family. Indeed, most of the women in the sample who had more than one or two children did not become active feminists until their children were old enough for school. Margaret MacDonald, who bore six children, is an exception, and the manner in which she combined her public and private life shows remarkable organising gifts and a strong sense of social commitment (MacDonald 1912, Herbert 1924).

The consequence, nevertheless, is that the women in the sample were not typical of the women of their period. They were more likely to be unmarried, and if they were married, more likely to be childless and less likely to have a really large family. The question that must be asked, therefore, is the extent to which this actually had an effect on their feminism and, because they were in large part the leaders of 'first-wave' feminism, on the nature and direction of the women's movement itself. To what extent, for example, did it ignore the needs of married women, and particularly the needs of mothers, in its concern for the problems faced by unmarried women?

This chapter on the relationship of the female sample with parents, siblings, husbands, and in some cases lovers, has been limited in its findings by the lack of information in a number of cases. At the same time, the very different patterns of relationships that were revealed indicate clearly the great variety of personal background to be found in this sample and the complexity of the process of becoming a feminist, a complexity which will be explored in greater detail in a later chapter. The purpose of the present chapter, as was the case with Chapter 2, has been to fill in the background from which the leading figures in 'first-wave' feminism were drawn. If the picture that has been revealed is far from a simple one, it has the merit of casting doubt on some of the stereotypes that have dogged the history of feminism. By the early twentieth century, for example, a substantial minority of the women coming into the movement were of working-class social origin. At the same time, the Liberal connection of 'first-wave' feminism has been over-drawn, and by the 1890s certainly it was socialism rather than Liberalism which was the dominant political affiliation, at least of the women in this sample. Free thought was associated with feminism but did not dominate it, and all the major denominations contributed to some extent to the making of feminism.

At the more personal level fathers appear to have had an unexpectedly large influence on their daughters. More unconventional, by and large, than mothers, they have been important in encouraging unconventionality in their daughters. Some of the women in the sample were on bad terms with one or even both their parents, and their rebellion against their parents was one aspect of their more general rebellion as feminists, but this was not the typical pattern. We need, therefore, to explore the possibility that feminism was itself an expression of a more general attitude to reform held by men who were not necessarily feminists themselves.

At the same time, the stereotype of feminists as spinsters is also untrue. The majority of the sample were, or had been, married at the time of their involvement in the women's movement. Nevertheless, unmarried women represented a very large and significant minority in the sample as a whole which in cohorts I and IV became the majority. It is difficult under such circumstances to avoid the supposition that unmarried women were a significant influence on 'first-wave' feminism although the nature of that influence has still to be determined. Nor, in spite of well-known examples like Caroline Norton, Anna Wheeler and Annie Besant were the women in the sample unhappily married. Indeed a number of their husbands were themselves active in the women's movement.

It will be the purpose of the next chapter to explore some of the findings in this and the previous chapter in relationship to particular feminist campaigns. The argument, therefore, will move from the personal and social characteristics of 'first-wave' feminists in general, to the characteristics of the women involved in the major campaigns which make up the women's movement during this period. Once again this is a question that has not previously been asked in this form and the findings should enable a new and different light to be thrown on the campaigns themselves and, even more significantly, the manner in which the different campaigns were related to each other. An examination, in some detail, of the subsequent history of cohort IV, the last generation of 'first-wave' feminism, will also, it is hoped, shed further light on the decline of the women's movement in the years after the vote was won.

4 The Women's Movement

This chapter will be concerned with the major campaigns which occupied the women's movement during the years between 1850, when feminism as an organised movement may be said to have begun, and 1930 when what has been described as 'first-wave' feminism was drawing to a close. Eight campaigns have been selected as representing the several different aspects of the movement over time, namely, women's suffrage, the repeal of the Contagious Diseases Acts, legal rights for married women, better educational and employment opportunities for girls and women, birth control, the women's trade union movement, and family allowances. These campaigns have all been described elsewhere, and this is not the place to repeat that description in detail. Nevertheless, for the benefit of readers not well acquainted with the history of the women's movement in Britain, a brief account of each campaign has been attempted here.

The suffrage movement is the best known and best documented aspect of 'first-wave' feminism (Fulford 1956, Rover 1967, Liddington and Norris 1978, Morgan 1975a, Rosen 1974, Garner 1983). Its origin as an organised campaign did not occur until the 1860s although it was claimed by feminist writers as early as the 1820s (Thompson 1825). By the early twentieth century it had come to dominate the whole women's movement, as the vote came to be seen as the key to all the other reforms women wanted to achieve for themselves and for others. The tactics of the militant suffrage campaign added their own appeal and for the only time during its history 'first-wave' feminism took on many of the characteristics of a mass movement. Victory was finally achieved in 1928, although by 1918 the granting of the vote to the majority of women took most of the urgency out of the campaign. The issue of women's suffrage was therefore not only a long and hard-fought campaign but one which in the final resort ended in victory, and it will be suggested later that both the characteristics of the campaign itself and its successful conclusion played a part in the decline of the women's movement after the vote was won.

The campaign to improve the education of girls and women may be said to have begun with the foundation of Queens College in 1847. Intended primarily to improve the education of governesses and teachers, it was to provide the opportunity of a limited form of higher education for several women in the sample. During the 1850s progress was slow, but opinion was gradually changing and by the 1860s the existence of a growing number of good schools for girls, as well as the inclusion of girls' schools in the investigation of the Schools Enquiry Commission, paved the way for an effective system of secondary education for middle-class girls. At the same time, beginning in the 1870s, the university system was gradually opened to girls and women (Burstyn 1980, Stephen 1927, Ellsworth 1979, Kamm 1958, Tullborg 1975). By the end of the century, therefore, if opportunities for middle-class girls were by no means equal to those of their brothers, the situation had improved dramatically, as the change in the educational background of the female sample between cohort I and cohort IV makes abundantly clear.

The allied cause of better employment opportunities for women may be said to have originated with the foundation in 1859 of the Society for the Promotion of the Employment of Women. The main aim of the campaign was the widening and improving of the opportunities for women in skilled and professional employment and its activities ranged from the printing trades to the medical profession (Strachey 1928, Holcombe 1973). At the same time there was opposition to attempts to remove women from certain occupations on the grounds that they were dangerous or immoral (John 1984) and, in the twentieth century in particular, opposition to the marriage bars, especially in teaching and the Civil Service

(Lewenhak 1977, Soldon 1978). Although certain limited objectives were reached, most notably perhaps the opening of the medical profession to women, and although the occupations open to women, especially in clerical work, did in fact improve during this period, this is an aspect of 'first-wave' feminism which seems to have retained its vitality throughout the whole of the period of this study and indeed beyond it.

The campaign for the legal rights of married women was the subject of the very earliest feminist victory in 1839 when Caroline Norton was successful in her attempt to improve the position of a wife with respect to the guardianship of her children, and the issue of legal rights remained central to 'first-wave' feminism for the rest of the century. In the early 1850s the petition to give married women the right to own their own property, organised largely under the guidance of Barbara Bodichon, marked the start of what was to be a persistent effort to change the law and which only ended with the Married Women's Property Act of 1882. In 1886 the Custody of Infant Acts improved the custody rights of mothers, although their position was still not equal and this particular campaign continued into the 1920s and beyond. The other main issue concerned the grounds of divorce which, according to the 1857 Act, made adultery grounds for divorce for a husband but not for a wife. This issue was finally settled in 1923. Most of the aims of the campaign for legal rights for married women, at least as they were formulated within 'first-wave' feminism, were, therefore, eventually achieved (Holcombe 1983).

The campaign against the Contagious Diseases Acts was an important area of feminist action between 1870 and the repeal of the Acts in 1886, although there was a brief revival in the 1890s when there was a proposal to impose similar legislation in India. Intended to protect the Armed Forces against venereal disease, the Acts provided for the forced examination and, if necessary, compulsory treatment of women believed to be prostitutes. Originally confined to garrison towns, it was the decision to extend the Acts which brought about a large-scale campaign for their repeal. The attack on the Acts was made on a number of grounds, including the erosion of civil liberties that they entailed as well as a moral objection to the implicit assumption that prostitution was necessary. The specific feminist case rested mainly on the double standard of sexual morality which the Acts not only assumed but indeed enshrined. By concentrating on the prostitute and not on her client the Acts, it was claimed, ignored not only the extent to which prostitutes were the victims of what was essentially male lust, but also the part played by low wages and poor employment opportunities in forcing girls into prostitution. By explaining prostitution as a consequence of both the sexual and the economic exploitation of women the Contagious Diseases controversy significantly widened the meaning of 'first-wave' feminism and, although the controversy itself was short-lived, it is too important an aspect of the nineteenth-century women's movement to be excluded for that reason (Walkowitz 1980).

The birth control campaign on the other hand is much less easy to place within feminism. Although a number of feminists, like Frances Wright for example and, in a later generation Annie Besant, supported birth control as a way of freeing women from constant child-bearing, most feminists, right up until the end of the century, shunned the birth control movement (Banks and Banks 1964). With the new century, however, ideas were changing, and by the 1920s, if still somewhat cautiously, feminists began to campaign for the extension of birth control knowledge to the women of the working classes. Part of a greater appreciation, by this time, of women's own sexual needs, this was also influenced by the widespread anxiety at the high level of maternal and infant mortality within the working classes (Ledbetter 1976, Lewis 1980, Leathard 1980).

The next campaign to be considered, the women's trade union movement, reflects a growing interest on the part of feminists in the earnings and working conditions of women industrial workers. The movement owes its origin to Emma Paterson who, in 1874, founded the Women's Protective and Provident League, later the Women's Trade Union League, with the object of drawing women into the trade union movement (Goldman 1974). By the 1890s there were several organisations concerned specifically with the welfare of women workers, and a programme which involved a policy of legislation to protect women from exploitation at work (Lewenhak 1977, Soldon 1978, Mappen 1985).

The final issue, family allowances, is essentially a twentieth-century development, and has been included as an example of the 'new feminism' which, under the leadership of Eleanor Rathbone, began to win support during the 1920s (Lewis 1973). Based initially on the separation allowances paid during the First World War, it was attractive to a number of feminists because, provided it was paid to the mother, it would help to weaken women's economic dependence on their husbands. It is of particular interest, therefore, in so far as it went beyond the idea of legal equality in the feminist attempt to change the balance of power within the family.

The first step in the analysis in this chapter is to chart the amount of support which these particular campaigns received from the women in the sample. Support has been defined in terms of some active involvement, whether this was collecting signatures for petitions, serving on a committee, speaking at meetings, chairing meetings, or contributing to written propaganda in the form of articles or pamphlets. This information is given in Table 12 according to cohort. Since many women were involved in more than one campaign, two totals have been given for each cohort, namely, the total number of women involved in each campaign, and the total number of women in the cohort. The percentages, however, refer to the proportion *in each cohort* involved in each of the campaigns. In this way it is possible to make a comparison across the cohorts, and so indicate the change in support for each campaign over time.

The average number of campaigns in which the women were involved is 2.5, although the spread was wide, ranging from one to five. There was some variation between cohorts with involvement highest in cohort II (2.7) and lowest in cohort IV (2.1), but the differences were very small and followed no particular pattern. Turning now to look at the particular campaigns, the dominance of suffrage is immediately apparent. Overall, it involved 89% of the sample, a proportion far greater than for any other campaign, reaching a level of 96% in cohort III. Support for suffrage is lowest

Table 12: Involvement of female sample in women's movement campaigns, by cohort

	Cohort I		Cohort II		Cohort III		Cohort IV		Total	
	No.	%	No.	%	No.	%	No.	%	No.	%
Suffrage	20	77	20	95	24	96	23	86	87	89
Education	15	58	12	57	2	8	0	0	29	30
Employment	12	46	9	43	12	48	12	46	45	46
Legal rights	11	42	5	24	5	20	3	12	24	24
C.D. Acts	8	31	4	19	1	4	0	0	13	13
Birth control	1	4	3	14	7	28	8	31	19	19
W.T.U. movement	0	0	4	19	8	32	3	12	15	15
Family allowances	0	0	0	0	3	12	6	23	9	9
Total	67		57		62		55		241	
Total in cohort	26		21		25		26		98	

in cohort I and this indicates a certain degree of caution in some of the first generation of feminists when it came to the suffrage issue. Anna Jameson, for example, although she was prepared to challenge male domination in both the family and in employment, believed that politics would always remain a masculine domain (Thomas 1967). Others in cohort I, initially equally cautious, later changed their minds. The two Shirreff sisters, for example, believed, in 1849, that man's political and even his domestic domination was an aspect of the natural order that should not, and indeed could not, be changed, but by 1870 they were active propagandists for women's suffrage (Ellsworth 1979). By the second generation this caution with respect to women's political rights seems to have disappeared and they were beginning to be accepted as the most basic and necessary rights of all.

The decline in support for the suffrage campaign in cohort IV is at first sight, perhaps, surprising but represents the belief of some socialist feminists that the claim for women's suffrage should be made only as part of an adult suffrage bill. This was not a general belief amongst socialist women (Liddington and Norris 1978), and it was not shared by most of the socialist feminists included in this study. It was, however, sufficiently widespread to cause considerable controversy both within feminism and within the Labour movement (Banks 1981), and the two points of view are well expressed in the public debate between Margaret Bondfield and Teresa Billington-Greig in 1907 (Bondfield 1949).

No other campaign was given the same level of support, but the issue of better employment opportunities came closest, both in terms of its overall support (45%) and the fact that it maintained its importance throughout the whole period of the study. Even in cohort IV the issue commanded the support of twelve women, 46% of the cohort, and a level of support higher than that for any other campaign except suffrage. Better employment opportunities, therefore, may be said to have been a key theme throughout 'first-wave' feminism, second only to women's suffrage.

No other issue achieved this level of support overall, largely because no other issue was significant for so long.

The campaign for better educational facilities, for example, involved only 30% of the sample as a whole, but 58% of cohort I, and 57% of cohort II. Indeed in both these cohorts the educational campaign commanded more support than any other issue except suffrage, including the issue of employment opportunities. Thereafter, however, it declined very swiftly, almost certainly because the immediate goals of the campaign had been largely realised. Between cohort I and cohort IV, for example, the number of women achieving some form of higher education rose from three to sixteen. In the field of employment opportunities success had proved harder to achieve, especially in the professions. Some, like the Church, were still altogether closed to women and opportunities for advancement for women were limited everywhere. The imposition of marriage bars, especially in teaching, also provided new goals for women's groups to fight for, and this remained a live issue until such barriers were formally ended at the close of the Second World War.

Another issue which was important to the first generation of feminists but not to later generations was the campaign for married women's legal rights. Involving as many as 42% of cohort I, it declined gradually over time, although it did not disappear entirely even in cohort IV. This decline undoubtedly reflects the actual successes which occurred during the nineteenth century, especially in the area of property and earnings and, to a lesser extent, the guardianship of children.

The same is true of the campaign against the Contagious Diseases Acts which lasted less than twenty years before the repeal of the Acts brought it to a close. Individual feminists like Josephine Butler herself (Butler 1898) continued to work in this general area, and there was a brief campaign in the early years of the twentieth century against the light sentences given to child molesters (Linklater 1980), but these did not assume the same significance within feminism as the campaign against the Contagious Diseases Acts, which involved, as Table 12 shows, 31% of cohort I and a further 19% in cohort II.

The remaining three campaigns are significant not because they involved large numbers of women, but because they became important in the later stages of 'first-wave' feminism at a time when some of the earlier issues were losing their appeal. Involvement in the women's trade union movement, for example, is largest in cohort III, at which time as many as 32% of the sample are involved in it. The campaign for birth control, however, shows a steady increase in significance which reaches its peak in cohort IV. The family allowance campaign also reaches its peak in the last cohort, where it claims 23% of the sample.

Clearly, therefore, we are faced with a considerable change of emphasis as we move in time from cohort I to cohort IV. The only stable features are suffrage and the campaign for better employment facilities for women. Several issues of particular concern to the first generation of feminists, like better education for girls and legal rights for married women, have lost their significance, and new issues, like birth control and family allowances, have taken their place. It has been suggested that some issues lost their appeal largely because the original goals of the women's movement—for better schools for example, or for an end to the legal dependence of married women—had been, in large part at least, achieved by the end of the nineteenth century. There may be other reasons, however, associated with changes in the social background of the sample and its political affiliation, and these changes may also have played their part in the selection of new feminist goals. It is to this consideration that the analysis now turns.

There was little difference between the groups in terms of their level of involvement. It was highest in the business group (2.87) but the professional group and the working-class group were identical (2.25). Moreover, women from the working classes were represented in every campaign without exception, although they are clustered in suffrage, in employment opportunities and in the women's trade union movement. Their involvement in the suffrage movement is, however, lower (81%) than any other group although it is, of course, at a very high level still. At the same time 44% of working-class women were part of the women's trade union movement, a considerably higher level of involvement than in any other group. At the other extreme, they were considerably less likely to have been

Table 13: Involvement of female sample in women's movement campaigns, by social origin

	Gentry		Professional		Business		Working class		Not known		Total
	No.	%	No.	%	No.	%	No.	%	No.	%	No.
Suffrage	9	90	32	89	28	93	13	81	5	83	87
Education	6	60	10	28	11	37	1	6	1	17	29
Employment	5	50	15	42	17	57	7	44	1	17	45
Legal rights	2	20	10	28	9	30	2	13	1	17	24
C D Acts	3	30	3	8	5	17	2	13	0	0	13
Birth control	2	20	3	8	9	30	2	13	3	50	19
W T U M	0	0	4	11	4	13	7	44	0	0	15
Family allowances	0	0	4	11	3	10	2	13	0	0	9
Total	27		81		86		36		11		241
Total in group	10		36		30		16		6		98

Note: The percentages are calculated in terms of the total in the group involved in the educational campaign, or in the campaign for the legal rights of married women. It should be noticed, however, that because the number of working-class women is so small they were in the minority in every single campaign. This is true even of the women's trade union movement, where eight of the fifteen were from a middle-class background, and seven from the working classes. The family allowance movement too, although designed to benefit working-class mothers, was predominantly a middle-class movement and so, to an even greater extent, was the birth control movement. The lack of involvement of working-class women in the campaign for better educational provision is understandable when we recall the extent to which it was concerned with middle-class educational provision. Moreover this campaign, like the campaign against the Contagious Diseases Acts, was fought at a time when there were very few working-class women in the women's movement.

It is not easy to determine how far changes in the social origin of the female sample, and more especially the decline in the gentry and the increase in working-class women described in Chapter 2, was responsible for the change of emphasis within feminism itself. Both the gentry and the working class are small groups, outnumbered by women from business or professional families so that any influence they may have had could not have been a large one. Moreover, even in the women's trade union movement, where the influence of working-class women was at its highest, more women, so far as this sample is concerned, were from a middle-class than a working-class background. Even the family allowance movement was, in its leadership certainly, predominantly middle-class. It is necessary, therefore, to go beyond the change in the social background of 'first-wave' feminism and to examine those circumstances which not only brought more working-class women into the movement but changed the orientation of middle-class women themselves.

For the purpose of Table 14 the sample has been divided into three categories: socialist, non-socialist, and no known political affiliation. It should be pointed out that those with no known political affiliation are very unlikely to have been

Table 14: Involvement of female sample in women's movement campaigns, by political affiliation

	Socialist		Non-socialist		No known political affiliation		Total
	No.	%	No.	%	No.	%	No.
Suffrage	39	87	28	93	20	87	87
Education	5	11	15	50	9	39	29
Employment	16	36	13	43	16	70	45
Legal rights	9	20	10	33	5	22	24
C D Acts	1	2	8	27	4	17	13
Birth control	10	22	5	17	4	17	19
W T U M	15	33	0	0	0	0	15
Family allowances	7	16	2	7	0	0	9
Total	102		81		58		241
Total in group	45		30		23		98

socialist, but for the sake of accuracy they have been kept apart from those with a specific political affiliation whether this was Liberal or Conservative. As in previous Tables in this Chapter the percentages have been calculated in terms of the total in each group.

Socialists were involved in every single campaign, and non-socialists in every campaign except the women's trade union movement, which was exclusively socialist. Socialists, however, were involved in fewer campaigns on average (2.27) than either the non-socialists (2.7) or those with no political affiliation (2.52). Nevertheless the difference is a small one. Socialists were mainly uninvolved in the campaign against the Contagious Diseases Acts, perhaps because this was over before the move towards socialism began and, perhaps for the same reason, the campaign for better education and the campaign for legal rights for married women. The family allowance campaign was, however, largely in the hands of socialists, who were also just slightly in the majority in the birth control movement. Moreover, in spite of socialist reservations with respect to the campaign for a limited suffrage bill, socialist women were well represented in the suffrage campaign. Indeed, of the total of 87 women in the sample involved in this campaign, as many as 39 were socialist in their political affiliation.

To a large extent the preoccupations of socialist women were the same as those of working-class women, but this is not because socialist women were necessarily working-class in their background. Middle-class socialist women also shared in the concern for the needs of working-class women and, as Table 13 showed, were well represented even in the women's trade union movement. The family allowance movement too, as has been shown, was led mainly by middle-class rather than working-class socialists. The change in emphasis in feminism, therefore, reflects the move within feminism towards a socialist political philosophy which re-interpreted feminist goals in what was perceived to be the interests of working-class women. In this move the women's trade union movement appears to have played a decisive part, producing a collaboration between middle- and work-ing-class women which acquainted middle-class women with the actual realities of working-class life and turning them, or many of them, into socialists. At the same time the middle-class women recruited working-class women who were already socialists into feminism.

Table 15: *Involvement of female sample in women's movement campaigns, by religious affiliation*

	Positive religious affiliation		Freethinker		No known religious affiliation		Total
	No.	%	No.	%	No.	%	No.
Suffrage	33	85	27	87	27	96	87
Education	13	33	12	39	4	14	29
Employment	17	44	12	39	16	57	45
Legal rights	8	21	10	32	6	21	24
C D Acts	6	15	6	19	1	4	13
Birth control	4	10	8	26	7	25	19
W T U M	6	15	3	10	6	21	15
Family allowances	4	10	2	6	3	11	9
Total	91		80		70		241
Total in group	39		31		28		28

In this table all those with a positive religious affiliation have been grouped together, but freethinkers have been kept separate from those with no known religious affiliation even though they are certainly closer to the freethinkers than to the rest. Percentages have been calculated in terms of the total in each group. In fact, however, the differences between the three groups are small and do not reveal any clear pattern. It is not unexpected to find those with a positive religious affiliation underrepresented in the birth control movement, which was for a long time linked with the secularist movement. Indeed, many religious groups were opposed to contraception even in the 1920s. More unexpected, perhaps, is the prominence of freethinkers in the campaign against the Contagious Diseases Acts, which had very strong moral overtones and a great deal of religious support (McHugh 1980). Campaigns which show a some-what unexpected level of involvement from those with a positive religious affiliation include the women's trade union movement and the campaign for family allowances. Both are late developments in 'first-wave' feminism, at a time when positive religious affiliation was declining, and the women's trade union movement in particular had a high proportion of working-class women, only one of whom had a positive religious affiliation. In other words, it was the middle-class socialist feminists who held positive religious beliefs.

Perhaps the clearest conclusion to be drawn from the table as a whole is the extent to which both freethinkers and those with a positive religious affiliation were allies in the various campaigns of the women's movement. Although there were differences of emphasis, the predominant impression is that differences in religious affiliation were less significant than differences in political affiliation in the general pattern of feminist involvement. In no sense can any of the campaigns be described as a simple reflection either of free thought or of religious belief although some, like birth control, come closer to it than others. Religion could provide the motivation for feminist involvement, as it did, for example, for Josephine Butler and indeed for Florence Nightingale (Boyd 1982), but religious women like Josephine Butler worked for the repeal of the Contagious

Diseases Acts alongside freethinkers like Ursula Bright and Emilie Venturi (Walkowitz 1980), and this was true to a greater or lesser extent for every single one of the campaigns that have been examined in this study. Moreover, although a positive religious affiliation declined over time and was more frequent amongst non-socialist than socialist feminists, it did not disappear altogether. It was still to be found amongst middle-class socialists, although rarely amongst socialists from a working-class background. It remained, therefore, a significant if diminishing aspect of the feminist tradition throughout the whole of 'first-wave' feminism even after it had been overtaken by socialism.

Table 16: Involvement of female sample in women's movement campaigns, by educational experience

	Some higher education		No higher education		Total
	No.	%	No.	%	No.
Suffrage	32	94	55	86	87
Education	9	26	20	31	29
Employment	16	47	29	45	45
Legal rights	7	21	17	27	24
C D Acts	1	3	12	19	13
Birth control	10	29	9	14	19
W T U M	6	18	9	14	15
Family allowances	8	24	1	2	9
Total	89		152		241
Total in group	34		64		98

Note: Percentages have been calculated in terms of the total in each group.

Because the women with some higher education increased very considerably over time, educated women tend to cluster in the later rather than the earlier campaigns. It is not particularly surprising therefore to find the campaign for the repeal of the Contagious Diseases Acts almost entirely in the hands of women without higher education. An exception is the campaign for better education for girls, which was also an early campaign but which did manage to attract a large number of educated women. Of course the number of women without higher education is almost twice as large as those who had attended college or university, so that in most of the campaigns women without higher education are in the majority. The exceptions are the birth control campaign, where women without higher education are just outnumbered, and the family allowance movement which was in fact almost entirely in the hands of university graduates.

Table 17: Involvement of female sample in women's movement campaigns, by marital status

	Married		Ummarried		Widowed etc.		Total
	No.	%	No.	%	No.	%	No.
Suffrage	39	93	39	87	9	82	87
Education	13	31	12	27	4	36	29
Employment	22	52	19	42	4	36	45
Legal rights	8	19	9	20	7	46	24
C D Acts	6	14	6	13	1	9	13
Birth control	10	24	8	17	1	9	19
W T U M	8	19	6	13	1	9	15
Family allowances	3	7	5	11	1	9	9
Total	109		104		28		241
Total in group	42		45		11		98

Note: Percentages have been calculated in terms of the total in each group.

Married women engaged in more campaigns (2.60) than unmarried women (2.31) but the difference was small. It is also very clear from the table that married and unmarried women were not involved in a radically different pattern of campaigns. Even issues like improved educational and employment opportunities which were largely in the interests of single women, involved unmarried and married women in virtually equal numbers. The legal rights of married women also gained the support of unmarried as well as married women. Moreover, the order of importance of the campaigns is also strikingly similar for the two groups. Only the very small group of widowed and separated wives shows a somewhat different pattern, in their greater proportional involvement in the battle for the legal rights of married women. The large number of unmarried women active in 'first-wave' feminism does not appear to have had any substantial effect on the pattern of their campaigns, in which married and unmarried women seem to have shared on virtually equal terms.

Table 18: Involvement of female sample in women's movement campaigns, by marital experience

	Successful		Unsuccessful		Total
	No.	%	No.	%	
Suffrage	24	92	16	89	40
Education	10	38	4	22	14
Employment	16	62	8	44	24
Legal rights	9	35	6	33	15
C D Acts	3	12	1	6	4
Birth control	5	19	4	22	9
W T U M	3	12	4	22	7
Family allowances	3	12	1	6	4
Total	73		44		117
Total in group	26		18		44

Unmarried women have not been included in Table 18. Nor have the small number (9) of married women whose marriages have not been classified as successful or unsuccessful due to lack of information. Women with successful marriages were involved in rather more campaigns (2.8) than women with unsuccessful marriages (2.44) but the difference was small. Nor was the pattern of involvement itself strikingly different. Even the issue of the legal rights of married women was as important to women with successful as with unsuccessful marriages, even though separated wives are included in the unsuccessful group. Indeed, because the number of marriages classified as unsuccessful was small, more of the women working for legal rights for married women were in fact happily rather than unhappily married. The example of Caroline Norton, whose unhappy marriage led her to work for the rights of mothers to the custody of their children (Holcombe 1983) must be contrasted with that of Ursula Bright, whose marriage appears to have been an exceptionally happy one (Bright

1936) but whose main life work was in the field of married women's property and earnings (Holcombe 1983).

In examining the background characteristics of this sample of active feminists in terms of their involvement in particular campaigns, political affiliation has emerged as by far the most important. The change in emphasis which occurred in feminism at about the turn of the century is closely matched by the change in political affiliation at that time, and it is impossible to avoid the connection between them. Although socialist and non-socialist women shared some concerns, and most notably issues of women's employment and the demand for women's suffrage, the 'new feminism' which developed was closely, although not exclusively, linked to the spread of socialism within the feminist movement.

An examination of single campaigns conceals the extent to which the campaigns were linked together by means of a common, or at least an overlapping, membership. Most women were involved in more than one campaign, some indeed in several, so that it has been possible to explore the extent to which women in any one campaign were also involved in each of the others, and this is set out in Table 19. For simplicity, percentages rather than numbers have been used, and these should be read downwards. For example, 31% of the women involved in the sufrrage campaign were also in the education campaign, 45% in the campaign for better employment opportunities, and so on.

The most striking thing about this table is the extent to which women in all the other campaigns were also involved in the suffrage struggle. The chief exception was the women's trade union movement, some of whom had reservations not about suffrage itself but about the value to working-class women of a suffrage campaign based on a limited suffrage. No other campaign had nearly so wide an appeal, and there were also a number of suffrage supporters, especially during the latter part of the campaign, who were involved in no other issue. Almost half the suffrage workers, however, also took part in the campaign for better employment facilities, nearly a third in the education campaign, and nearly a quarter in the campaign for legal rights.

There were close links also between the educational

Table 19: *Percentage of female sample in each campaign involved in each of the other campaigns*

	Suffrage	Education	Employment	Legal rights	C D Acts	Birth control	W T U M	Family allowances
	%	%	%	%	%	%	%	%
Suffrage	–	93	87	86	85	95	73	89
Education	31	–	36	36	62	16	0	0
Employment	45	55	–	46	38	42	33	67
Legal rights	24	31	24	–	46	21	7	33
C D Acts	13	28	11	25	–	5	7	0
Birth control	21	10	18	17	8	–	20	22
W T U M	13	0	11	4	8	16	–	44
Family allowances	9	0	13	13	0	11	27	–

campaign and the campaign for better employment opportunities. Indeed as many as 55% of those working for better education for girls were also working for wider employment for women. Legal rights, too, also had close links with both education and employment, and these three issues had, to a very considerable extent, an interlocking membership during the latter half of the nineteenth century when, along with suffrage, they formed the backbone of the women's movement.

The controversy centring on the Contagious Diseases Acts was, as has been shown, a short-lived campaign and, in the sample as a whole, involved only thirteen women. Nevertheless, it was not isolated from the rest of the women's movement. It had close links with suffrage and with the legal rights movement, and, most surprisingly of all, perhaps, as many as 62% of the women involved in the Contagious Diseases Acts controversy were also involved in the campaign for better education for girls and women. The birth control movement too, if to a lesser extent, also had ties with the rest of the women's movement. Although early pioneers like Annie Besant were isolated from the mainstream, by the 1920s those women who took up the cause of birth control had close links with other aspects of the women's movement.

The women's trade union movement was the most isolated. Its closest ties were with women's suffrage, and after that with issues concerning women's employment and, to a lesser extent, family allowances. Its links were small with most of the mainstream issues of the nineteenth-century women's movement including education, legal rights and the Contagious Diseases Acts campaign. Although already active as early as the 1880s and 1890s, its ties were therefore very much with the 'new' rather than the 'old' feminism. There were links for example, with the birth control movement, and with the campaign for family allowances. The family allowance campaign itself was less isolated from the mainstream of feminism, but the table reveals the extent of its ties to the women's trade union movement.

Table 19, therefore, presents a picture of a social movement which was more than a series of single campaigns.

Although there were significant changes over time, which are reflected clearly in the absence of relationships between what were essentially nineteenth-century campaigns and those which emerged in the twentieth century, there was a great deal of overlapping and it was not unusual for a woman to be involved in three, or even in some cases four, different campaigns during her life-time.

The table also makes clear, however, the extent to which the suffrage issue dominated the whole of 'first-wave' feminism. It was not only the campaign which involved the largest number of women in the sample, it was also closely related to all the otherampaigns to an extent considerably beyond that of any other issue. As many as 95% of women in the birth control movement were also in the suffrage campaign, and so were 93% of those working in education. The lowest relationship was with the women's trade union movement, but even in this case as many as 75% of those in the women's trade union movement also worked for women's suffrage. Because the suffrage was seen as the means to achieve all the claims made by 'first-wave' feminism it became over time not just one feminist goal amongst others, but the central core of 'first-wave' feminism, which helped to unify it as a social movement.

This is not to imply that there were no divisions within the suffrage movement. Indeed, almost from the start there were rivalries between different factions, including a brief but painful dispute between those who wanted to include married women in a proposed suffrage bill, and those who did not (Rosen 1974). But the most significant was the conflict, already referred to, between those who wanted to wait for adult suffrage and those who were prepared to accept a suffrage bill which would have enfranchised only those women with property of their own (Banks 1981). Perhaps the best known conflict occurred between the constitutionalists and the militants, a dispute it should be emphasised that was solely to do with tactics. Originally the suffrage campaign had been strictly constitutional, relying mainly on political lobbying with particular emphasis on gaining the support of the Liberal Party. It was the gradual loss of confidence in this approach that led, after 1900, to the introduction of more militant methods, and eventually to actual violence. Feminists from both the militant and the constitutional wings were included in the sample in sufficient numbers to make a comparison possible between them, and the significance both of the suffrage issue and this particular dispute within the suffrage movement seemed to make the comparison worthwhile.

Although there were clearly militants and constitutionalists in the sample it was not always simple to categorise a woman as one or the other, since women tended to change sides, either from a constitutional to a militant position or, even, the other way round. Any woman who spent a number of years in the militant wing was classified as a militant even if she later changed her mind. Moreover, the militant wing was defined to include not only the Women's Social and Political Union but the somewhat less militant Women's Freedom League. Less violent in its tactics, it nevertheless pursued unconstitutional methods, including a refusal to pay rates and taxes. In accordance with this scheme of classification, there were 26 women in the sample in the militant group and 32 in the constitutional group, a rather surprising finding when it is remembered how much greater impact the militants had, both in their own time and on the impressions of subsequent generations.

It is sometimes assumed that the constitutionalists and militants were very different from each other, but in fact the comparison made here shows them to have been in many respects very similar. Five of the militants (19%), compared with six (19%) of the constitutionalists were of working-class social origin. On the other hand, the constitutionalists were more aristocratic with 13% from the gentry, compared with only 4% for the militants. Perhaps this was because the militant Women's Social and Political Union had originated within the Independent Labour Party, whereas the constitutionalists, in the National Union of Women's Suffrage Societies, were traditionally Liberal in their political allegiance. Indeed socialists were well represented in the militant group, making up as many as 62%. They were not, however, far behind amongst the constitutionalists where they made up as many as 50%. Other differences between the two groups were also fairly small. The constitutionalists, for example, were more likely to be freethinkers, with 31% in this category compared with only 25% of the militants. The constitutionalists were also better educated, with 50% having experienced some form of higher education, compared with 42% of the miltants.

What chiefly differentiates the two groups, however, is the extent to which they were involved in other feminist issues. All but one of the constitutionalists had taken part in at least one other feminist campaign, and several in more than one. Eleven of the militants however (42%) were involved only in suffrage. Most of these were young women drawn in by the excitement of militancy and, for several years at least, the suffrage campaign was their life. But once the vote was won (Kenney 1924), or indeed, in some cases, once the militant campaign came to an end in 1914 (Hesketh 1966), interest was lost in the whole issue of feminism. The constitutionalists, in contrast, contained a high proportion of older women with experience of the women's movement going back, in some cases, to the 1870s or even earlier. The significance of militancy, therefore, was its success in appealing to women who had no previous commitment to feminism. Drawn in specifically by the dramatic appeal of militancy, and particularly its leaders, their level of involvement is not in question. Indeed a number of them were quite prepared to give their lives for the cause, and one of them at least, Emily Wilding Davison, did so (Colmore 1913). Moreover, the very nature of militancy meant that they had to make great sacrifices in their personal lives as well as having to endure the physical suffering of a prison sentence. In many cases, nevertheless, their enthusiasm for feminism did not long survive the ending of militancy.

It is worthwhile in this connection to consider briefly the record of involvement of all the women in cohort IV in the period after 1918. All were born between 1872 and 1892 so that even the oldest of them might have been expected to play some part in events during the 1920s, and indeed, of the 26 women in this group, fifteen continued, for a time at least, to be involved actively in the women's movement. Of the eleven who dropped out, one was dead, but of the rest eight had been militants and only two constitutionalists.

This retreat from active feminism, and in a number of cases even from sympathy with feminism, had complex causes and cannot be easily explained here. Some of the women, like Mary Blathwayt for example (Dobbie 1979), simply returned to their private lives from which the excitement and comradeship of militancy had briefly drawn them. Others moved in a completely different intellectual direction. Christabel Pankhurst herself started a new and successful career as a Second Adventist (Mitchell 1977a). Edith Rigby, another militant who had thrown herself with total commitment into the suffrage cause, now became equally absorbed in the ideas of Rudolf Steiner and, indeed, in later life came to regret her involvement in the suffrage movement (Hesketh 1966). Clearly these were women for whom the more mundane levels of political life had, and could have, no appeal. Moreover, for some of them at least it is likely that the intellectual content of feminism did not go very deep.

Nevertheless, too much should not be made of this retreat from feminism. During the 1920s a useful nucleus of women remained, both constitutionalists and militants, and several new recruits were drawn in like Dora Russell (Russell 1975). One important feminist group centred around Margaret Thomas, Viscountess of Rhondda, a former militant and owner and editor of *Time and Tide* which, during the 1920s, was an important outlet for feminist ideas (Spender 1984). Margaret Thomas herself was also largely responsible for two new organisations founded during the 1920s, the Open Door Council and the Six Point Group, both concerned largely with equal employment opportunities for women.

Another centre of activity during the 1920s was the National Union of Societies for Equal Citizenship, formerly the National Union of Women's Suffrage Societies, which included amongst its most active members women like Eva Hubback, Eleanor Rathbone and Mary Stocks. This organisation was responsible for several important legal changes, including equal divorce rights and improved custody rights for mothers (Hopkinson 1954). NUSEC was also part of the campaign for family allowances under the leadership of Eleanor Rathbone (Stocks 1949). The 1920s also saw the move to provide birth control information for working-class women, spearheaded by women like Marie Stopes (Hall

1977), Stella Browne (Rowbotham 1977) and Mary Stocks (Stocks 1970).

The 1920s, therefore, were by no means years of decline even if they did not match the excitement and commitment of the suffrage campaign. It was only during the 1930s that the picture really changed. Women, even those who had been very active during the 1920s, moved away from feminism into other areas of concern so that by the end of the 1930s very few in this last generation of 'first-wave' feminists were active in feminist politics. Marie Stopes, for example, had by this time lost most of her interest in the birth control movement, and instead cultivated a literary salon to which she invited writers like H. G. Wells, Hugh Walpole and Lord Alfred Douglas (Hall 1977). Eva Hubback, during the 1920s the efficient and dedicated Parliamentary Secretary to the National Union of Societies for Equal Citizenship, turned during the 1930s mainly to other issues, most of which had little to do with feminism. Moreover, by the 1940s some of her ideas on motherhood were closer to the feminine mystique of the 1950s than to feminism (Hopkinson 1954).

Even more significant than the gradual withdrawal of feminist activists from the women's movement was the failure to recruit a new generation of young women to become the future leaders. If the pattern established during the nineteenth century had continued a new generation of women, born approximately between 1895 and 1915, would have been recruited and would in time have become the new feminist leaders in the 1930s and 1940s. Some women born in this period did indeed come forward in the 1920s, and women like Vera Brittain, Rebecca West and Winifred Holtby joined with an older generation of feminists like Lady Rhondda, Elizabeth Robins and Cicely Hamilton in the circle of feminists grouped around *Time and Tide*, but, sadly, *Time and Tide* drifted away from feminism to become an arts and literary review (Spender 1984). Dora Russell, perhaps the most important new recruit to feminism during the 1920s, also drifted away from active feminism, becoming absorbed eventually in the peace movement. Some women, like the MP Edith Summerskill for example, did remain deeply committed to feminist issues (Summerskill 1967), but in this respect she was exceptional amongst the women in Parliament (Vallance 1979).

If we try to examine the reason for the state of doldrums into which feminism seems to have fallen during the 1930s prominence must be given to the belief, shared by many of the feminists themselves, that the major battle had been won. Mary Stocks, for example, a lively and radical feminist as late as the 1920s, came to believe this at the end of her life, and in 1970 declared that 'I am no longer a member of an unprivileged sex' (Stocks 1970). Moreover, this attitude seems to have been held by much younger women. In 1952 Marghanita Laski could say, 'Older and nobler women struggled so that I could be free, and did their work so well that I've never even bothered about being bound' (Doughan 1980). Other women, still believing in a woman's movement, redefined its objectives. By 1938, for example, Eva Hubback was arguing that peace was the first objective of the women's movement, followed by the 'preservation and welfare of our racial stock'. The more traditional concern of feminism, putting an end to what she called the 'remaining inequalities' between men and women was relegated to the third and last place.

This is not to suggest that feminism came to an end during the 1930s. The equal pay issue continued to command the attention of many women, especially in the trade union movement (Lewenhak 1977) and was indeed to increase in importance during the war years (Smith 1981). Women's groups also continued to oppose the marriage bar (Soldon 1978). Some new issues were also raised. In 1936, for example, the Abortion Law Reform Association was founded by a group of feminists among whom Stella Browne was perhaps the most important (Hindell and Simms 1971). Another important pressure group during the war years was Women for Westminster which campaigned for improved access by women to the political process (Wilson 1980). There was also a short-lived and unsuccessful attempt during the war to press for an Equal Citizenship (Blanket) Bill which would have made sex discrimination unlawful, and this anticipated by thirty years the provisions of the 1975 Act (Doughan 1980).

By this time, however, the women's movement had been

fragmented into a series of small pressure groups, sometimes working in uneasy harmony but as often in opposition to each other. Women industrial workers, for example, tended to see feminist pressure groups like the Open Door Council as representing middle-class interests, ignoring the needs of working women. The equal pay struggle, too, which was probably the most important of all feminist campaigns during this period, also divided women along class lines (Smith 1981).

Unlike 'first-wave' feminism, therefore, which was united by what was in some respects a joint leadership, and by the issue of suffrage, which acted as a powerful unifying force, the years after 1930 saw the women's movement dissolve into a number of small pressure groups pursuing different aims against a background which was either unsympathetic to feminism altogether or adopted the view that the main objectives of the women's movement had already been won and that women were both free and equal. Those women who throughout this period still thought of themselves as underprivileged because they were women suffered from feelings of isolation and indeed of oppression. As Elizabeth Wilson has argued, during these years feminism 'led an underground or Sleeping Beauty existence in a society which claimed to have wiped out that oppression' (Wilson 1980, p. 187).

There were, however, other reasons for the decline in feminist activity during the 1930s which are concerned with changes within feminism itself, and particularly those changes in feminist ideology which paralleled the move from a political orientation which was largely Liberal to one that was predominantly socialist. It is significant, for example, that twentieth-century feminism turned away from the issues that had most involved nineteenth-century feminists to concentrate upon a new set of issues that had hardly concerned nineteenth-century feminists at all. This was not simply because certain limited goals, like the entry of women into the medical profession, had been achieved but rather the substitution of new goals altogether, consequent upon a wholly different feminist ideology. It is with this change in the ideological aspect of feminism that the next chapter is concerned.

5 Feminist Ideology

Behind the struggle to achieve feminist goals lies a set of beliefs about the relationships of men and women, both as they are perceived to be in reality and as they should be, which can most conveniently be described as the ideology of feminism and which is both the cause and the justification of the campaigns themselves. It is the purpose of this chapter to examine the ideas about feminism held by the individual women in this study, and in this way to build up a picture of feminist ideology both as it changed over time and in its relationship to the personal and social characteristics of 'first-wave' feminists themselves.

First, however, it is necessary to describe the categorisation used in the analysis. This has been based on the ideas expressed by the women directly in articles, books, pamphlets and letters as well as in reports of speeches and lectures. An attempt has been made to select the most frequently expressed themes, so that the categorisation reflects as far as possible the women's own assumptions and beliefs. In some cases there was insufficient evidence to make any categorisation possible, but this was rare. Naturally enough, most women fall into more than one ideological category and where this has occurred they have been classified under more than one heading. The analysis in this chapter therefore follows the same pattern as in Chapter 4, except that the categories used refer not to campaigns, but to ideological positions. Altogether, nine different positions have been distinguished which appear to represent different aspects or facets of feminist ideology as it was conceived by the women in the sample.

The first category, labelled 'unmarried women' in each of the tables, includes all those arguments which justified particular claims on the basis of the needs not of women generally, but of unmarried women. These needs might be conceived of mainly in financial terms, as when employment opportunities were demanded for girls or women forced by economic necessity to support themselves in the absence of a husband or father. A good example of this position is provided by Bessie Rayner Parkes, later Mrs Belloc, who argued that since women increasingly have to be their own breadwinners it is only just that opportunities should be provided for them to do so (Parkes 1866). At other times, as in the writings of Emily Shirreff for example, the emphasis was less on economic necessity than on the need for unmarried women to lead useful and satisfying lives (Shirreff 1858). Essentially this was a claim on behalf of the spinster, that women who did not marry should be able to live useful and happy lives, and as a significant corollary that women should not be forced into unsuitable marriages because no alternative way of life was open to them.

The second category, labelled 'autonomy', refers to the revolt against the traditional view enshrined in customs, religion, and the law itself that women did not exist in their own right but only in relationship to men, whether as mother, daughter, wife or mistress. It argued instead that women needed and deserved both identities and destinies of their own. In the words of Frances Power Cobbe, woman was created not for 'the service she can render to man', but 'for some end proper to herself' (Cobbe 1869). The most vivid expression of this point of view is provided by Cicely Hamilton in her lively book *Marriage as a Trade* (Hamilton 1909), but it was also a significant aspect of the feminism of Elizabeth Robins (Robins 1924). Believing that women's dependence had crippled them emotionally, intellectually and morally, Cicely Hamilton anticipated some of the ideas of modern feminism in her critique of the part played by the ideology of romantic love in keeping women in their place. This view is above all a cry for independence and the recognition of women's rights as individuals. Although applicable especially to the women who did not want to marry, it was essentially a demand for autonomy for all women, single or married.

The third category, labelled 'double standard', refers to the opposition to the double standard of sexual morality which was the driving force behind the campaign against the Contagious Diseases Acts but which also determined the attitude to prostitution, venereal disease, and the sexual abuse of women. Although influenced strongly by the concepts of justice and equality, in so far as it was a demand for equal standards of morality to be applied to men and women, it was not a claim for equal rights with men. There was hardly any demand from women for sexual freedom for women during the whole period of 'first-wave feminism' even on the part of Owenite feminists (Taylor 1983), and the freedom enjoyed by men was seen as a licence which allowed men to express their sensuality at the cost of the sexual exploitation of girls and women. Opposition to the double standard, therefore, was a drive to enforce on men the standards hitherto imposed only on women. Indeed, in the sample as a whole, only four women wanted more sexual freedom, three of them in cohort IV, and it was left to a later generation to equate sexual freedom with women's emancipation. Indeed when, in 1911, the short-lived feminist journal *The Freewoman* advocated sexual freedom for women (Garner 1983) the response from many leading feminists was of unmixed horror. Olive Schreiner, writing to Havelock Ellis in 1912, condemned it as the voice 'of the brutal self-indulgent male' and argued that, far from expressing what women were fighting for, it expressed exactly what they were fighting against (Cronwright-Schreiner 1924).

The opposition to the double standard, therefore, was largely a protest against women's sexual exploitation by men, whether this was expressed in the general toleration of male sexual self-indulgence by both public opinion and the courts, in the physical abuse of women by men, or in a legal system which condemned the prostitute and protected her client. Christabel Pankhurst's pamphlet *The Great Scourge and how to end it*, originally published as a series of articles in *The Suffragette*, is a good example of the way in which feminist thinking linked venereal disease with women's economic and political subjection. Although Christabel exaggerated the extent of venereal disease in the population, and her remedy—that women should refuse to marry—was an extreme one, there is no doubt from the evidence of this study that many women were frightened by the knowledge, often new to them, that a man could infect both his innocent wife and their children. It is not altogether surprising, therefore, that so many feminists came to believe that if women had the vote they would put an end to prostitution. Opposition to the double standard, therefore, was primarily concerned with freedom from sexual oppression and sexual exploitation (Jeffreys 1982, Coveney 1984).

The next category, 'equal marriage', is also a somewhat complex set of attitudes. A reaction against the doctrine of women's subordination in marriage, it replaced the traditional patriarchal and essentially hierarchical view of marriage with the concept of a partnership which, even if it allowed for very considerable differentiation of role or what Josephine Butler, somewhat romantically, called a 'sweet interchange of services' (Butler 1869) was nevertheless essentially egalitarian rather than authoritarian in its view of the husband/wife relationship. It expressed on the one hand a dislike if not an actual fear of marriage as it existed, under law, which put women almost entirely in the power of their husbands and on the other an idealised view of the blissful union that marriage might become, if male domination and female dependence were replaced by a relationship based on equality.

A further category, 'economic independence', has been used to group together those women who believed that women's dependence in marriage was ultimately economic in nature. Consequently changes in the law were insufficient to protect women, so long as they were dependent economically on their husbands. This group of women advocated the provision of an independent source of income for wives, either by bringing them into the work force on equal terms with men, or by the provision of some sort of state support for mothers. By realising the limitations of legal equality these women were more radical than those who believed that equality in marriage could be brought about by changes in the law alone.

The category 'co-operative house-keeping' is also more radical in its implications than 'equal marriage'. Placing emphasis mainly on the inequalities inherent in the division of labour in the home, the remedy is seen as some form of communal provision of services for housework and child care. In this way the wife and mother can be freed from the master/servant relationship inherent in the domestic arrangements of the private household.

The category 'mothers and children' involves an acceptance of the view that women are first and foremost mothers, and challenges only the conditions under which women, and especially working-class women, are forced to carry out this role. Primarily concerned with the concept of welfare, it is essentially a demand that greater resources should be made available to mothers, whether in the form of grants and allowances, better facilities for the training of girls as mothers, or an improvement in the health facilities available for mothers and their children. Sometimes, although not always, associated with eugenic principles, it revealed itself in a concern, like that expressed by Eva Hubback, for example, for the preservation and welfare of the racial stock (Hopkinson 1954).

The next category, 'complementary roles', depended upon an acceptance of distinctive roles for men and women based primarily on women's actual or potential maternity. Coming close in some respects to traditional ideas on femininity, it did not, however, accept either the necessity of women's subordination in the home, or her exclusion from the public sphere. Indeed frequently, as in the case of Josephine Butler for example, it was argued that women were needed in public life specifically because they were different from men. In the home, and in public life, she believed, men and women played different but essentially complementary roles (Butler 1869).

The final category, 'protection', represents a view of women at the opposite pole in many ways to the category 'autonomy'. Like the previous category 'complementary roles' it takes a largely traditional view of women, emphasising their need for protection rather than their desire for independence. Like the category 'mothers and children', it was brought into play mainly in connection with working-class women, and especially the industrial worker, and took the form, in the main, of attempts to control the hours and conditions of work of women in industry as well as attempts to prohibit women from certain dangerous trades altogether.

If we look first at the final column, the overall total in each ideological category, we see that 'autonomy' occurs most frequently, a confirmation of the significance within 'first-wave' feminism of women's desire for independence and a life of their own. It reflects the importance of the equal rights tradition within feminism with its emphasis on individuality and personal liberty. The next frequent category, more surprisingly, is the 'double standard'. Clearly, the existence of a double standard of sexual morality pressed heavily on these women and, although the campaign against the Contagious Diseases Acts involved only a small number of women for a short time, the attitude of mind that it expressed was very widespread within 'first-wave' feminism. At the other extreme both 'co-operative housekeeping' and 'protection' represent very much minority points of view with the rest of the categories in an intermediate and roughly similar position.

It is the comparison over time, however, which gives this table its greatest interest. It will be seen at once that both the category 'autonomy' and the category 'double standard', the two most frequent ideological categories overall, have declined quite substantially over time. 'Autonomy' is still a significant element in feminist ideology even in cohort IV but by no means the most important, and the decline in significance of opposition to the double standard, which has fallen steadily from 50% in cohort I to 19% in cohort IV, is even more marked. It is the category of 'unmarried women', however, which has experienced the greatest decline, from 50% in cohort I to 4% in cohort IV. The category 'equal marriage' has also declined in importance, although to a much less marked degree, and 'complementary roles' is less significant in cohorts III and IV than in cohorts I and II, although the difference is not very great.

It is obvious, therefore, that the shape of feminist ideology has changed very considerably over time. The most important categories in cohort I have all become less significant, and the category 'unmarried women', so important

Table 20: Feminist ideology of female sample, by cohort

	Cohort I		Cohort II		Cohort III		Cohort IV		Total
	No.	%	No.	%	No.	%	No.	%	No.
Unmarried women	13	50	10	48	3	12	1	4	27
Autonomy	11	42	10	48	11	44	6	23	38
Double standard	13	50	8	38	8	32	5	19	34
Equal marriage	7	27	7	33	7	28	3	12	24
Economic independence	4	15	2	10	5	20	9	35	20
Co-operative housekeeping	3	12	0	0	2	8	5	19	10
Mothers and children	1	4	2	10	8	32	13	50	24
Complementary roles	7	27	6	29	3	12	5	19	21
Protection	0	0	2	10	3	12	2	8	7
Total	59		47		50		49		205
Total in cohort	26		21		25		26		98

Note: Percentages have been calculated in terms of the total in each cohort.

in both cohort I and cohort II, has virtually disappeared altogether. At the same time certain other categories have become increasingly important. The most significant of these is the dramatic increase in the category 'mothers and children', which interestingly almost exactly parallels the decline in the category 'unmarried women'. Indeed it is tempting to see the concern for mothers and children actually replacing the concern for unmarried women as one of the major themes in feminist ideology. Certainly in cohort IV the concern for mothers and children was undeniably the major theme overshadowing all the rest. In this respect it mirrored a general anxiety in Edwardian Britain and throughout the 1920s and 1930s at the high level of infant and maternal sickness and mortality, shared by feminists and non-feminists alike (Harrison 1981) just as in the mid-nineteenth century there was a widespread concern, not necessarily feminist in its implications, for the problem of the so-called surplus women (Banks and Banks 1964).

Another category which shows an increase over time is 'economic independence'. From one of the smallest categories in cohorts I and II, it is, by cohort IV, at 35% second in importance only to the category 'mothers and children'. This clearly represents a more radical approach to marriage within twentieth-century feminism. On the other hand, the category 'co-operative housekeeping' shows no such pattern. Always the response of a small proportion of women, it actually declines over time, reflecting the loss of interest in Owenite communitarianism. There is a revival of interest in cohort IV, representing less a belief in community living than in state-provided child care services, but it is still, at 19% a minority point of view. Perhaps this reflects the availability of some form of domestic assistance, even if only on a limited scale, even to some women in the working classes. Ada Chew, for example, used her earnings to pay someone to look after her daughter (Chew 1982). It is also worth noting that the possibility of a greater involvement on the part of a husband in the care of house and children hardly entered the minds of 'first-wave' feminists. Margaret Bondfield, as a young woman, painted a picture of an ideal marriage in which husband and wife shared the household tasks between them, but the article, published in

1898, roused a storm of protest and she never returned to this conception of marriage (Hamilton 1924). The only other advocacy of this solution occurs in an article by Ray Strachey in 1936 (Strachey 1936). Otherwise 'first-wave' feminism seems to have accepted without question the sexual division of labour in the home.

The category 'complementary roles' also represents a minority view in 'first-wave' feminism, but one which becomes less rather than more important over time. Nevertheless, the decline is not very large and this view was still held by as many as 19% of cohort IV. It was not, therefore, associated only with the early stages of feminism when the concept of sex equality was still a novelty, but persisted into the twentieth century.

The category 'protection' is also a minority view within 'first-wave' feminism and one which increases rather than declines over time, although only to a very small extent. Indeed, most 'first-wave' feminists were deeply opposed to any attempt to place restrictions on female labour, and when in 1886 and 1887 efforts were made to outlaw the pitbrow women, who performed a variety of jobs above ground at British coal mines, the leaders of the women's movement, including Lydia Becker, Helen Blackburn, Jessie Boucherett and Josephine Butler, fiercely opposed the proposed legislation (John 1984). Indeed, as late as 1896, Jessie Boucherett and Helen Blackburn published an unequivocal attack on all protective legislation (Boucherett and Blackburn 1896). The Women's Trade Union League, too, was, at the time of its origin, opposed to protection for women industrial workers but, in the years that followed, the League itself changed its mind. By the twentieth century feminists like Gertrude Tuckwell, Mary Macarthur, Margaret MacDonald and Margaret Bondfield had come to see protective legislation as a major factor in improving the working conditions of women in industry. In 1902, for example, Margaret MacDonald, at a meeting of the National Union of Women Workers, raised the issue of women working in bars. Convinced that the work was degrading, attempts were made, under her leadership, to introduce legislation prohibiting the employment of barmaids, although existing jobs were to be safeguarded

(MacDonald 1912). This attempt failed, but protective legislation for women remained trade union policy after the First
World War, approved by women trade unionists themselves
(Banks 1981). Table 20 shows that it was a minority view
in every cohort, but its presence within 'first-wave' feminism
was not only a divisive factor within feminism itself but
helped to split the women's trade union movement from
those feminists opposed to the concept of protection.

If we look at the table as a whole, therefore, it is obvious
that feminist ideology changed considerably even within the
period of 'first-wave' feminism. The concern with unmarried
women, so prevalent in the first cohort, virtually disappeared, and issues like autonomy and the double standard
became considerably less important. Nor was this simply
because the problems which concerned the early feminists
had been solved. To some extent this was true, but most of
the issues raised by the double standard of sexual morality
were as important for women in the twentieth century as in
the nineteenth century, as the modern feminist movement
has discovered for itself. By cohort IV the emphasis was on
a completely new set of problems, of which the concern
with the welfare of mothers and children was the most
important. In order to explore some of the possible reasons
for this change, Table 21 examines the relationship between
feminist ideology and political affiliation. Percentages have
been calculated in terms of the total in each group.

It is difficult to avoid the conclusion that the change in
feminist ideology was in large part at least a consequence
of the change in political affiliation that occurred within
feminism during the last decade of the nineteenth century.
By cohort III the majority of women were socialists and the
Liberal/feminist alliance was over. The effect of this change
is clearly mirrored in Table 21, which shows that socialist
women had a different pattern of ideologies from other
women, and that it was largely socialist women who
provided support for those ideological categories, like the
welfare of mothers and children, which characterised twentieth-century rather than nineteenth-century feminism. Thus
47% of socialist women supported the ideology 'welfare of
mothers and children', and only 10% of all other women.
They were also much less likely than other women to

Table 21: Feminist ideology of female sample, by political affiliation

	Socialist		Non-Socialist		No known affiliation		Total
	No.	%	No.	%	No.	%	No.
Unmarried women	4	9	11	37	12	52	27
Autonomy	14	31	15	50	9	39	38
Double standard	14	31	12	40	8	35	34
Equal marriage	12	24	8	27	4	18	24
Economic independence	11	18	7	23	2	9	20
Co-operative housekeeping	8	18	0	0	2	9	10
Mothers and children	21	47	3	10	0	0	24
Complementary role	8	18	8	27	5	22	21
Protection	7	16	0	0	0	0	7
Total	99		64		42		205
Total in group	45		30		23		98

support the ideology 'unmarried women' as well as 'autonomy' and 'the double standard'.

On the other hand, socialist feminists do not appear to have been more radical as feminists than other women. Although dominating the category 'co-operative house-keeping', they were less likely proportionately to support the economic independence of wives than were non-socialist women. Moreover, although less likely to support the ideology of 'complementary roles', the difference was a relatively small one. Similarly, the category 'protection' which is based on traditional definitions of women as the weaker sex is, as the table shows, supported *only* by socialist women. The most important characteristic of the ideology of socialist feminists has indeed less to do with gender than with social class, and the socialist women stand out from the rest by virtue of their deep concern for the welfare of working-class women whether they were industrial workers, or wives and mothers at home.

At the same time, and perhaps even more significantly, there was a decline in the essentially liberal doctrine of autonomy and its associated belief in the removal of restrictions on individual freedom. In its place was a very decided move towards collectivism, including a collective solution to women's problems. This change in emphasis was well expressed by Enid Stacy, a feminist lecturer for the Independent Labour Party during the 1890s, who claimed that the rise of socialism within feminism has made feminists turn away from individualism to the idea of social duties based on the importance of wifehood and motherhood (Stacy 1897). Indeed socialist feminists, like other socialists, appear to have accepted fully the ideas of collectivism as an organising principle of social life and turned to the state to provide women with the resources they needed to raise the status of working-class women and particularly working-class wives and mothers. This contrasts with much nineteenth-century feminism which was concerned to free women from the restrictions placed upon them by both law and custom and which opposed the influence of the state in women's lives even when its declared aim was their protection. The change in feminist ideology therefore was part of a much wider change in political attitudes as the Labour Party replaced the Liberal Party as the main vehicle of reform.

A further consequence of the acceptance by feminists of a socialist point of view was to move economic exploitation to the centre of the stage. All oppression was now seen as economic in origin, so that other forms of exploitation, including gender exploitation, were seen primarily in economic terms. While this had certain clear advantages in leading feminists to understand, for example, the limitations of legal changes alone, it meant that forms of sexual exploitation which were not primarily economic in nature, like the sexual abuse of children, were neglected. Even more significant for feminism was the central place given in socialist theory to the issue of social class. By defining the exploitation and oppression of working-class women as social class exploitation, the extent to which middle-class women were oppressed as women was ignored and, even more significantly, so was the extent to which working-class women were exploited by reason of their gender by men, including *husbands*, in their own class. It was this attitude, above all, which allowed men and some women too to believe that sex should be kept out of politics.

A further question to be asked is the extent to which these changes reflected the increase in the number of feminists of working-class origin. Table 22 therefore examines feminist ideology in relation to social origin. For the sake of simplicity the six women of unknown social origin have been omitted. Percentages have been calculated in terms of the total in each group.

It is immediately apparent that, although the small group of women in the gentry are very different, women of working-class origin are on the whole very similar to women of the middle classes. This is most obvious with respect to the category 'mothers and children' which, if usually set in the context of working-class needs, appealed equally to middle-class and to working-class women; but even the category 'protection', if exclusively socialist, was by no means confined to working-class women. Nor was the other predominantly socialist category 'co-operative house-keeping'. Although both these categories were proportionately more frequent in the working class, the difference was slight, and in numerical terms, because the proportion of working class in the sample was small, the majority of women falling into these categories was middle-class. Nor were the working-class feminists more likely than middle-class feminists to support the economic independence of wives. It is true that certain categories significant to the upper and middle classes, like 'unmarried women', the 'double standard' and even 'equal marriage' were less significant to women of the working class, but they were just as likely as middle-class women, though not women of the gentry, to support the category 'autonomy'. The changes of emphasis within feminism, therefore, must be attributed to a change in the attitude of middle-class women, rather than to an increase in the proportion of working-class women within the women's movement. Indeed it will be suggested subsequently that the change in the attitude of middle-class feminists, and especially their interest in socialism, was itself one factor in the rise in the number of working-class women in the movement.

Table 22: Feminist ideology of the female sample, by social origin

	Gentry		Professional		Business		Working-class		Total	
	No.	%	No.	%	No.	%	No.	%	No.	
Unmarried women	7	70	14	39	4	13	2	13	27	
Autonomy	7	70	12	33	13	43	6	38	38	
Double standard	4	40	11	31	13	43	4	25	32	
Equal marriage	2	20	10	28	9	30	2	13	23	
Economic independence	1	10	7	19	7	23	3	19	18	
Co-operative housekeeping	0	0	4	11	1	3	2	13	7	
Mothers and children	0	0	11	31	7	23	4	25	22	
Complementary role	4	40	11	31	4	13	1	6	20	
Protection	0	0	3	8	1	3	2	13	6	
Total	25		83		59		26		193	
Total in group	10		36		30		16		92	

An examination of the association between religious affiliation and involvement in feminist campaigns revealed that,
although religious affiliation did influence feminist involvement to some extent, it was much less significant than
political affiliation in explaining changes in feminist involvement over time. It is now necessary in Table 23 to examine
the connection between religious affiliation and feminist
ideology. Percentages, as in previous Tables, have been
calculated in terms of the total in each group.

*Table 23: Feminist ideology of female sample, by religious
affiliation*

	Positive religious affiliation		Free-thinker		No known religious affiliation		Total
	No.	%	No.	%	No.	%	No.
Unmarried women	18	46	6	19	3	11	27
Autonomy	11	28	15	48	12	32	38
Double standard	13	33	16	52	5	18	34
Equal marriage	5	13	12	39	7	25	24
Economic independence	8	21	6	19	6	21	20
Co-operative housekeeping	2	5	7	23	1	4	10
Mothers and children	10	26	6	19	8	29	24
Complementary role	14	36	2	6	5	18	21
Protection	4	10	2	6	1	4	7
Total	85		72		48		205
Total in group	39		31		28		98

Freethinkers stand out for their support of the category
'autonomy', which was 48% of the group, compared with
only 28% of those with a positive religious affiliation and
32% of those with no known religious affiliation at all. It is
likely, however, that freethinkers in particular would prize
autonomy and independence so that the finding need cause
no particular surprise. More unlikely is the very strong
support (52%) amongst freethinkers for opposition to the
double standard of sexual morality which, it must be remembered, was not in general a plea for sexual freedom for
women, but the imposition of constraints on male sexuality

when it led to the exploitation of women. Those with positive religious affiliation also placed some but less emphasis on the double standard (33%), and it was those of no known religious affiliation who were relatively indifferent to the issue. The third category of importance to freethinkers was 'equal marriage' (39%). Here the contrast with those with a positive religious affiliation (13%) was very great, with those with no known religious affiliation in an intermediate position.

The most significant category for those with a positive religious affiliation was undoubtedly 'unmarried women'. This reflects the decline both in support for this category and in positive religious affiliation over time, but it may also signify a certain conservatism amongst religiously oriented women which is also reflected, for example, in their much greater tendency to support the category 'complementary roles'. As many as 36% in the religiously oriented group fall into this category compared with only 6% of freethinkers. They were also less likely to support co-operative housekeeping although not the economic independence of wives. Most interesting of all is the level of support for the category 'mothers and children' (26%) since this category, quite unlike the category 'unmarried women', is a late development within 'first-wave' feminism at a time when positive religious affiliation had declined.

Religious affiliation on the one hand, therefore, and free thought on the other, do appear to represent different traditions within feminism with significant implications for feminist ideology. Those with a positive religious affiliation placed less emphasis on equal rights, and more emphasis on those issues which may be defined as welfare, whether of unmarried women or, later, of mothers and children and it is this emphasis on welfare which probably explains their support for the economic independence of wives. Although some feminists saw this in terms of power, others, including many in the family allowance movement, saw it in terms of poverty. It is also not without significance that women with a positive religious affiliation were disproportionately represented in the category 'protection', which also took a traditional view of women.

Table 24: Feminist ideology and educational level of the female sample

	Some higher education		No higher education		Total
	No.	%	No.	%	No.
Unmarried women	8	24	19	29	27
Autonomy	10	30	28	43	38
Double standard	10	30	24	37	34
Equal marriage	5	15	19	29	24
Economic independence	12	36	8	12	20
Co-operative housekeeping	6	18	4	6	10
Mothers and children	14	42	10	15	24
Complementary roles	8	24	13	20	21
Protection	4	12	3	5	7
Total	77		128		205
Total in group	34		64		98

Note: Percentages have been calculated in terms of the total in each group

In general the educational level of the women in the sample did not make a great deal of difference to their feminist ideology. 'Autonomy' however was rated more highly by those without any higher education and so was 'equal marriage'. The biggest differences occurred with respect to 'mothers and children' in which women with some higher education not only gave much more support to this category proportionately but, in spite of their smaller number in the sample as a whole, were also numerically in the majority. The same is true of the category 'economic independence'. Indeed, for women with some higher education these are clearly the two most important categories of all. For women without higher education the two most important categories are 'autonomy' and the double standard of sexual morality.

To some extent this reflects the growth in educational provision, and the higher educational level of women in the cohorts III and IV, so that educated women naturally reflect the preoccupations of twentieth-century rather than nineteenth-century feminism. Hence their concentration in such categories as 'mothers and children' and 'economic independence'. It is not the whole story however. The categories 'unmarried women' and 'complementary roles' are both typical of early generations of 'first-wave' feminists, yet women with higher education are found in these categories in proportions little different from women without higher education. Indeed women with higher education are more likely to support the category of 'complementary roles'. The meaning of the table is, therefore, difficult to disentangle. Certainly it is possible to argue that women with education were less likely to value autonomy as a feminist goal because as educated women they had achieved greater independence for themselves, but this does not explain the difference between the two groups in categories like 'equal marriage' for example. Nor were educated women consistently more radical, even though they were more likely to support the category 'co-operative housekeeping', or less radical than other women. The table does, however, underline the extent in which educated women were part of the new, and largely socialist inspired, feminist ideology which characterised 'first-wave' feminism in the twentieth century. Of the 24 women supporting the ideology of the welfare of mothers and children, fourteen had had some higher education, mostly at university, and so had twelve of the twenty supporting the ideology 'economic independence of wives'.

Further light is thrown on these findings however if we look now at the relationship between married status and feminist ideology. Table 25 is based, as were previous tables, on marital status during the period of feminist involvement. Percentages have been calculated in terms of the total in each group.

Clearly there were differences in ideology between women of different marital status, although not always those that might be expected. Concern for unmarried women was, not surprisingly, greatest among single women, but the welfare of mothers and children was greatest among this group. Married women were most concerned with the issue of equal marriage and this was true particularly of separated wives. Married women were also more likely than unmarried women to emphasise autonomy, although the differ-

Table 25: Feminist ideology of female sample, by marital status

	Single		Married		Widowed or Separated		Total
	No.	%	No.	%	No.	%	No.
Unmarried women	17	38	9	21	1	9	27
Autonomy	16	36	18	43	4	36	38
Double standard	12	27	16	38	6	55	34
Equal marriage	6	13	12	29	6	56	24
Economic independence	7	16	10	24	3	27	20
Co-operative housekeeping	4	9	4	10	2	18	10
Mothers and children	13	29	9	21	2	18	24
Complementary roles	11	24	7	17	3	27	21
Protection	3	7	4	10	0	0	7
Total	89		89		27		205
Total in group	45		42		11		98

ence was fairly small, and to oppose the double standard of sexual morality. Single women were less likely to support the economic independence of wives, as well as complementary roles for men and women. The most frequently expressed ideological position for married women was autonomy (43%) and for single women, the status of unmarried women (38%).

Married women, therefore, were more concerned with the issue of marriage than single women, whereas single women formed the largest proportion of those who were concerned with unmarried women and their needs. On the other hand, single women were in the majority in the concern for mothers and children. It is possible, in this table, to identify an emphasis on the part of single women with needs, and married women with rights, especially if we take into account their greater concern with autonomy, but perhaps this is taking interpretation too far. It must also be noted that, although there are differences in emphasis, in no sense were certain issues confined to either single or married women. Even the category 'unmarried women' attracted 21% of the married women in the sample, and 'equal marriage' 13% of the single women.

Finally, it is possible to examine differences in ideology between women with successful and women with unsuccessful marriages. For the purpose of Table 26 widows and separated wives have been included, but single women and those who married after their feminist involvement was over have been excluded. Percentages have been calculated in terms of the total in each group.

Table 26: Feminist ideology and marital experience of female sample

	Successful		Unsuccessful		Not known		Total
	No.	%	No.	%	No.	%	No.
Unmarried women	6	23	3	17	1	11	10
Autonomy	10	38	9	50	3	33	22
Double standard	11	42	7	39	3	33	21
Equal marriage	10	38	5	28	2	22	17
Economic independence	7	27	6	33	0	0	13
Co-operative housekeeping	3	12	3	17	0	0	6
Mothers and children	8	31	2	11	1	11	11
Complementary roles	6	23	4	22	2	22	12
Protection	3	12	1	6	0	0	4
Total	64		40		12		116
Total in group	26		18		9		98

There are no large differences between women with successful and unsuccessful marriages. Those with unsuccessful marriages were more likely to fall into the categories of 'autonomy', 'economic independence' and 'co-operative housekeeping', but the differences were by no means large ones. Moreover, it was the successful marriages which were more likely to be associated with a concern for equal partnership in marriage. The welfare of mothers and children was also more likely to appeal to those with successful (31%) than unsuccessful marriages (11%). What is most evident from the table is the extent to which women whose own marriages were successful were nevertheless concerned with the reform of marriage. Indeed in a number of cases it seems to have been the success of their own marriage which led them to believe in the possibility of an equal partnership with men in marriage without the need for any very drastic re-assessment of marriage itself.

In order to take the analysis a stage further, feminist ideology has been related to involvement in the various campaigns of the women's movement and this is set out in Table 27.

The percentages in this table refer to the *rows* not the *columns*. Consequently row 1 gives information on the percentage of women in the ideological category 'unmarried women' who were involved in each of the eight campaigns that were included in the study. It is thus obvious that the category 'unmarried women' has its closest relationship with suffrage, in which 74% of the women were involved. This is followed by the employment campaign (59%) and better education facilities (52%). Women in this ideological category were relatively uninvolved in any other campaign and this underlines the extent to which the needs of unmarried women were seen largely in terms of improved facilities for education and employment. Indeed no other ideological category was so closely related to the campaign for better education. It is also significant that women in this category, although heavily involved in the suffrage issue, were less involved than women in any other ideological category with the exception of the small category 'protection'.

Women in the category 'autonomy' were more deeply involved in the suffrage movement (95%) than women in any other category with the exception of the category 'economic independence'. They were also the category with the highest involvement (66%) in the campaign for better employment opportunities. They also had a high involvement in the education campaign (37%) but this was less than the involvement not only of the category 'unmarried women' but also the category 'complementary roles' and the category opposition to the double standard. The only other campaign which involved more than a quarter of the women in this category was the legal rights campaign (29%). The analysis, therefore, brings out the extent to which, after suffrage, autonomy was seen in terms of education and employment opportunities for women, although legal equality in marriage was also important.

Table 27: Feminist ideology of the female sample and their involvement in the women's movement

	Suffrage		Education		Employment		CD Acts		Legal rights		Birth control		WTUM		Family allowances	
	No.	%	No.	%	No.	%	No.	%	No.	%	No.	%	No.	%	No.	%
Unmarried women	20	74	14	52	16	59	5	19	7	26	3	11	1	4	1	4
Autonomy	36	95	14	37	25	66	5	13	10	29	6	16	0	0	2	5
Double standard	28	82	13	38	13	38	13	38	15	39	6	18	1	3	2	6
Equal marriage	20	83	8	33	11	46	5	21	15	33	5	21	2	8	1	4
Economic independence	20	100	4	17	12	60	1	5	7	35	5	25	3	15	6	30
Co-operative housekeeping	9	90	2	20	2	20	0	0	1	10	1	10	1	10	1	10
Mothers and children	21	88	1	4	9	38	1	4	5	21	8	33	9	38	9	38
Complementary roles	17	81	8	38	8	38	4	19	8	38	3	14	3	14	3	14
Protection	3	43	0	0	2	29	1	14	1	14	1	14	6	86	1	14

The category of opposition to the double standard was
also linked most closely to suffrage (82%) but, interestingly,
this was followed in importance by the legal rights of
married women (39%), possibly because the marriage laws,
and especially the grounds for divorce which allowed
husbands to divorce their wives for adultery, but not wives
their husbands, was an obvious and indeed bitterly resented
aspect of the double standard. The campaign against the
Contagious Diseases Acts was also a campaign against the
double standard and this too was related closely to this
particular category (38%). On the other hand, women who
opposed the double standard of sexual morality were widely
dispersed in the women's movement, so that 38% were
also involved in the education campaign and 38% in the
campaign for better employment opportunities. Nothing
could better convey the centrality of opposition to the
double standard in nineteenth-century feminism.

'Equal marriage' was closely linked to suffrage (83%) and
to the legal rights campaign (33%) but also had a close
relationship with the campaign for better employment
opportunities (46%) and better education (33%). It was
therefore an essential element in equal rights feminism and
linked concern with the legal background to marriage with
the needs of unmarried women. In no sense was there a
division in 'first-wave' feminism between support for
married and support for single women.

The category 'complementary roles' also has its closest
links with the nineteenth century. After suffrage (81%) its
closest relationships are with the educational campaign
(38%), the employment campaign (38%) and the legal rights
of married women (38%).

The remainder of the ideological categories fall into a
somewhat different pattern of relationships. The economic
independence of wives, for example, although closely linked
with suffrage (100%), with better employment opportunities
(60%) and legal rights (35%), has only a limited relationship
with the education campaign (17%) and the campaign
against the Contagious Diseases Acts (5%). It does,
however, have closer links with the birth control movement
(25%) than any other ideological category except 'mothers
and children.' The same is true of its relationship to the

family allowance movement (30%). The category 'mothers and children' on the other hand, takes its place firmly within twentieth-century feminism. Still linked closely to suffrage (88%) and to employment opportunities (38%), both of which extended into the twentieth century, its closest links otherwise are with family allowances (38%), the women's trade union movement (38%) and the birth control movement (33%).

'Co-operative housekeeping', on the other hand is, with the exception of suffrage (90%), not closely linked with other aspects of the women's movement. This reflects the extent to which it failed to gain any real foothold in 'first-wave' feminism whether in the nineteenth century or early twentieth century. The category 'protection' is also relatively unrelated to the women's movement. Its closest relationship by far is with the women's trade union movement (86%) and even suffrage (43%) is linked to it at a level considerably below that of any other ideological category. The only other campaign to show more than a minimum level of relationships is employment opportunities (29%) and even that is below every other ideological category with the single exception of 'co-operative housekeeping'.

It seems, therefore, that in the early twentieth century feminism developed a different kind of emphasis which cut it off to some extent from its past. Whereas, in the nineteenth century, feminists from different intellectual traditions were able to work together for common goals, the changes in feminist ideology which, it has been suggested, were largely associated with the rise of socialism, led not only to a new set of goals but was ultimately to destroy 'first-wave' feminism itself.

A further analysis may be made by examining the relationship between the ideologies themselves, to see to what extent, and in what ways, they cluster together. This is set out in Table 28 which, for simplicity, is based only on percentages.

There are a number of interesting features about this table. If the category 'unmarried women' is examined, reading *downwards*, it will be seen that it is related most closely to 'autonomy', nearly half (44%) of the women

Table 28: *Percentage of female sample in each ideological category falling in each of the other categories*

	Unmarried Women	Autonomy	Double standard	Equal marriage	Economic independence	Co-operative house-keeping	Mothers & children	Complementary roles	Protection
Unmarried women	–	32%	29%	33%	5%	10%	8%	59%	14%
Autonomy	44%	–	38%	46%	30%	30%	17%	18%	0%
Double standard	37%	34%	–	67%	25%	60%	25%	53%	14%
Equal marriage	30%	29%	47%	–	100%	10%	17%	35%	14%
Economic independence	4%	16%	15%	0%	–	40%	21%	18%	0%
Co-operative housekeeping	4%	8%	18%	4%	20%	–	13%	0%	0%
Mothers and children	7%	11%	18%	17%	25%	30%	–	53%	86%
Complementary roles	37%	8%	26%	25%	15%	0%	38%	–	43%
Protection	4%	0%	3%	4%	0%	0%	25%	18%	–

falling into the category 'autonomy'. The other important issues for women in this category were 'complementary roles' (37%) and the 'double standard' (37%). It is not without significance, however, that 30% of the women in this category shared a concern for 'unmarried women' with a concern for 'equal marriage'.

The category 'autonomy' was found most frequently in association with the category 'double standard' (34%), but the category 'unmarried women' followed closely behind (32%), and so did the concept 'equal marriage' (29%). Even more significant is the absence of any association between the category 'autonomy' and the category 'protection', and the low association between 'autonomy' and 'complementary roles' (8%). That is to say, women who emphasised the need for autonomy and independence rarely believed in the need for complementary gender roles and tended to emphasise the similarities rather than the differences between men and women.

Those who believed in complementary roles were most frequently found in the category of 'unmarried women' (59%), illustrating the extent to which an emphasis on the needs of unmarried women could be combined with quite traditional views on the role of *married* women. Belief in complementary gender roles was also closely linked with opposition to the double standard (53%) and the welfare of mothers and children (53%). A combination of 'complementary roles' and 'equal marriage' was, however, by no means rare (35%), illustrating the extent to which equality in marriage, as in the case of Josephine Butler for example, did not rule out an equality based on difference rather than similarity.

Turning next to the category 'double standard', there is further evidence of the central role this ideology played in nineteenth-century feminism. It is particularly closely linked to 'equal marriage', where indeed the combination with the 'double standard' occurred more frequently than with any other. Indeed, the close connection between the two ideologies suggests the conclusion that what particularly concerned the women who combined these two ideologies was the need for a different kind of relationship in which domination is replaced by equality, and lust by love. For such women as these, the double standard of sexual morality was a threat to women not only outside marriage, but inside marriage itself. The relationship between the category 'double standard' and the category 'autonomy' is also high (38%), although there was also a somewhat lower relationship (26%) with the category 'complementary roles'. The category 'equal marriage' also appears, from this table, to have played a similarly central role. Women who fall into this category were also found very frequently indeed (67%) in the category 'double standard', the category 'autonomy' (46%) and 'unmarried women' (33%). At a lower level (25%) women in this category were also in the category 'complementary roles'.

It is clear, therefore, that particular ideological positions must be seen as falling into groups, rather than existing in isolation. Apart from the close links between the categories 'double standard' and 'equal marriage' they were in their turn linked to the category 'unmarried women'. 'Autonomy' and 'complementary roles' overlapped very little and appear to represent different traditions within feminism, but they both appeared in association with the categories 'unmarried women', 'double standard', and 'equal marriage', although in each case 'autonomy' appears to have been the more important element.

The next category to be considered, 'economic independence', was related closely to 'equal marriage' since all these women believed in this as an ideal, differing from those in that category only in their contention that it required economic independence for wives as well as equality in law. Otherwise the category had smaller links with other ideological categories. Its closest link, after 'equal marriage', was with 'autonomy' (30%) and this was followed by the 'double standard' (25%) and, more unusually, the 'welfare of mothers and children' (25%). This last relationship underlines the extent to which this was an aspect of twentieth-century rather than nineteenth-century feminist ideology, as well as the association between both these categories and the family allowance movement.

The category 'co-operative housekeeping' involved only a very small number of women but its relationship with other categories is nonetheless interesting. Clearly it was not independent and relates closely to such categories as the 'double standard' (60%), 'economic independence' (40%), 'autonomy' (30%) and 'mothers and children' (30%). There are on the other hand, no links with 'complementary roles', and very few with 'unmarried women'. It does seem to represent a more radical approach to feminism than other categories, and it is perhaps significant that of the total of ten women, two, Dora Marsden and Stella Browne, supported greater sexual freedom for women and were associated with the radical feminist journal *The Freewoman* (Garner 1983).

The last two categories, 'mothers and children' and 'protection', provide a different pattern of relationships. The highest relationship for 'mothers and children' is with 'complementary roles' (38%), underlining the extent to which this concept, although a late development in 'first-wave' feminism, retained traditional views on the differences between men and women, and particularly, in fact, on the importance to women of motherhood. This was followed in order of importance by 'protection' (25%) and the 'double standard' (25%). 'Autonomy' (17%) was considerably less important. 'Protection', on the other hand, is unique in terms of its complete independence from most other categories, including 'autonomy'. It does, however, have exceptionally close ties with 'mothers and children' (86%) and with 'complementary roles' (43%).

The material presented in this chapter reveals the extent to which, during the nineteenth century at least, feminists, even from very different intellectual standpoints, shared to a marked degree a common ideology which made feminism into a genuine social movement. Table 28, in particular, illustrates the extent to which different ideological categories overlapped, with 'double standard' and 'equal marriage' occupying a central place. By the end of the nineteenth century, however, the picture had started to change. There was a move away from autonomy, as part of the swing from individualism to collectivism and, as a corollary of this, a new emphasis on women's need for protection, whether as workers or mothers, rather than their desire for freedom from the restrictions which hampered their lives. At the same time feminists drew from socialism an awareness of class conflict and class interest which led them to a distrust of equal rights feminism, which they came to see, with a certain amount of justice, as representing mainly bourgeois women. In consequence, feminism became re-defined as the cause not of women in general, but of working-class women, and very little attention was paid to the ways in which gender can override differences of class background.

The new socialist feminism was however to prove, ultimately, a weakness rather than a strength. Family allowances, for example, which envisaged the support of children by the state rather than by their father, promised to free women from economic dependence on their husbands, and so remove them from what Eleanor Rathbone described as man's natural instinct for domination (Rathbone 1924). Yet at the same time it reinforced the view that a woman's place was in the home, and Maude Royden, for example, claimed that the scheme would remove thousands of married women from the work force (Royden 1917). In spite of its radical implications, therefore, it did nothing to break down the sexual division of labour in either the home or the workplace. Indeed, in many respects it tended actually to reinforce it. At the same time the family allowance movement lost its original feminist impulse and became submerged in other causes (Lewis 1973).

Apart from the family allowance movement which, by implication at least, was radical in its approach to marriage, most of the efforts to improve the welfare of women and children came to be concentrated on health and welfare provisions, like maternity and child welfare centres, free school milk, and better working-class housing. Although of benefit to working-class women, such provisions as these did nothing to change the balance of power within the family. Indeed by the 1940s the actual provisions of the welfare state in its family policy perpetuated the dependence of the wife on her husband by defining women as housewives and men as breadwinners (Wilson 1977, Land and Parker 1978). The same is true of family law which attempts to tie the support of wives and children to individual men and reinforces the idea of a woman's economic dependence (Brophy and Smart 1981).

The other ideological issue which proved dangerous to 'first-wave' feminism was protection. During the nineteenth century equal rights feminists were deeply opposed to protective legislation which was seen quite simply as an attempt to deprive women of the right to work. By the 1920s, however, the Labour and trade union movement was fully committed to a programme of protective legislation for women, and in 1927 the Women's Trade Union Conference fully endorsed this policy. In 1925, however, Viscountess Rhondda founded the Open Door Council to oppose all legislation which restricted a woman's right to work and which fought subsequently not only against such legislation, but also against marriage bars. The effect was to reinforce the cleavage within feminism across class lines. Although socialists like Emmeline Pethick-Lawrence supported the Open Door Council there was suspicion and even hostility between organisations representing industrial workers and equal rights feminists, as well as between industrial and white-collar organisations. Changes in feminist ideology, therefore, had a part to play in the failure of feminism to maintain itself as a united movement.

Moreover, in spite of its implicit feminist ideology, the British Labour movement was at best indifferent to the claims of feminism and at worst actively hostile to them. The best example of this hostility is the treatment accorded to those Labour women who tried, during the 1920s, to change the Labour Party's policy on birth control (Russell 1975, Leathard 1980). The significance of this debate does not lie only in the lack of sympathy shown by the male leadership to the women's views. Even more important was the division it produced among the women themselves. Marion Phillips, in spite of her feminism, proved a determined opponent, and Ellen Wilkinson, another feminist, was equivocal at best (Vernon 1982). Faced with the choice between their feminism and their socialism, these women, fearful of the risk to the Labour vote, turned their backs on the campaign.

The family allowances campaign also met with suspicion and even hostility from many sections of the Labour movement. It was seen as a threat to the principle of collective bargaining and even as an attempt to reduce wages, so that it was in fact opposed not only by many socialists, but even by socialist feminists on these grounds. Two of its early supporters, Gertrude Tuckwell and Ellen Wilkinson, were indeed later to turn against the policy for this kind of reason (Macnicol 1980). The concept of the family wage also went directly against the idea of family allowances. Basic to the family wage was the belief that a man's earnings should be sufficient to support an average family, including his wife and children, and the suggestion that children should be supported by the state rather than their father completely overturned this view. The acceptance, within the trade union movement in particular, of the concept of the family wage went further, however, than opposition to the idea of family allowances. It also played an important part in the general acceptance by the Labour movement of a concept of the welfare state which made the economic dependence of the wife a central plank of family policy.

The feminist policy of equal pay was also received equivocally within much of the Labour movement. Although equal pay was accepted in principle, this acceptance had less to do with feminism than with the natural trade union desire to eliminate women as a source of cheap labour. It was widely believed that this effect of equal pay legislation would be to drive women out of employment. On the other hand, if women were not replaced by men, the effect would be to threaten the principle of the family wage on which the whole concept of the male breadwinner depended. So male trade unionists were often anxious to perpetuate the wage differentials between male and female workers. Although there was pressure from women's organisations, especially during the years of the Second World War, they received no support from the Labour Party, and indeed Ernest Bevin played a dominant role in the opposition to the campaign on the grounds that equal pay would endanger industrial peace. Moreover, after the war the Labour government continued to oppose equal pay on the grounds of its expense (Smith 1981).

It is evident, therefore, that for socialist feminists there was always a strain between their socialism and their feminism, and indeed on most occasions they could press their specifically feminist goals only in opposition to the leadership of the Labour Party and the trade union movement. Socialist feminists were, therefore, constantly faced with the problem of reconciling their feminism and their socialism, a task which led them at times to abandon their feminism altogether. Alternatively, feminism was redefined in terms that could be accommodated within the more general goals of socialism.

It has already been suggested that the main tactic used by socialist feminists in their attempts to redefine feminist goals was the limitation of feminist concern to the needs of working-class women, and it is in this context that we must understand the emphasis given by socialist feminists to the ideological category 'women and children'. Even more significant, however, was the extent to which the needs of women and children were defined within a traditional view of the family which alone was compatible with the trade union belief in the family wage, and the patriarchal household based on the husband as breadwinner and the wife as mother and home-maker. Accordingly, feminist demands were concentrated on improving the position of women as home-makers, in such fields as housing and hygiene, and in support for measures like health centres to bring down the high rate of mother and infant mortality. Moreover, although it was recognised that women were needed in the public sphere of politics, this was mainly because of their experience of and interest in the private or domestic sphere (Rowan 1982). Although the socialist women supported family allowances in order to give mothers some income of their own, this was a controversial view within socialism. Moreover, even the family allowance movement believed very firmly that the destiny of most women was to be mothers and home-makers.

The attempt by British socialist feminists to harmonise class and sex by redefining feminism has its parallel in Europe where feminists who were also socialists had to meet very similar problems. Indeed, when faced with a choice between the goals and feminism and the needs of the class struggle, most European socialist feminists have in the past accepted the prior claims of socialism and postponed the struggle for the liberation of women until after the revolution. This has been in part an acceptance of a theoretical position which subsumes sexual inequality under the heading of existing property relationships, in part an emotional reaction to the specific problems of the working class. Attempts to raise feminist issues, like birth control for example and co-operative housekeeping, were, as in Britain, rejected by the socialist leadership as irrelevant or, as in Britain, electorally dangerous (Boer and Quotaert 1978).

The decline of 'first-wave' feminism, therefore, was in part at least a consequence of its alliance with socialism. Dissatisfied with the ideological emphasis of nineteenth-century feminism, socialist feminists were never able to harmonise adequately the competing claims of gender and class, and so were never able to develop an ideology of their own which would have been both socialist and feminist. Feminism was weakened both as a movement and as an ideology not only by the failure of the 'new feminism' to fulfil its early promise of a more radical approach to women's needs (Lewis 1973), but by the divisions within feminism that the opposition of class and gender made inevitable. The consequence was the fragmentation of the women's movement and the isolation of individual feminists both from each other and from the movement.

6 Men in the Women's Movement

Although there were a number of men who sympathised with the aims of 'first-wave' feminism, and lent it both encouragement and support in various ways, men did not as a rule play an active part in the women's movement, and its leadership from the first was in the hands of women. Perhaps the most striking thing about feminism is the extent to which it has been a movement *of* women and not just *for* women. This contrasts with the situation with respect to socialism which has always included amongst its leadership a high proportion from a middle-class rather than a working-class background. For reasons that are undoubtedly complex, men have never identified with the women's struggle in the way that both men and women have identified with the goals of socialism, and even men sympathetic to feminism have been content to let women do the fighting, in a way and to an extent that has never been true in the socialist movement. Nevertheless, although this is generally true, there have been from the first a number of men whose support for feminism went deeper than sympathy and who, by their actions, made a real contribution to the progress of 'first-wave' feminism. It is these men who form the male sample in this study.

The first point to notice is the small number of such men. There were only eighteen in the male sample, compared with the 98 women in the female sample. Moreover, not one of these men devoted his whole life to the women's movement in the way that was by no means uncommon in the women's sample. Even a man like John Stuart Mill was an active feminist only towards the end of his long life; and,

106

even for this group singled out for their unusual degree of commitment to feminism, the women's movement was only one of several causes to which they contributed their time and energy.

The very paucity of men who could be described as active rather than passive feminists makes this particular group more rather than less interesting, both in terms of the kind of contribution they were able to make, and the source of the motivation that drew them into an active identification with the women's cause. The small number makes it impossible to make the kind of quantitative analysis that was used with respect to the female sample so that, although the framework of analysis is similar, the main emphasis will be on a comparison with the female sample, rather than on an analysis of the male sample itself. In making this comparison, however, it should be kept in mind that, whereas the female sample is distributed equally between the four cohorts, this is not true of the male sample. As many as 39 of the men were in cohort I, and only one man in cohort IV, a reflection of the gradual decline in male support for the women's movement over time.

One reason for this decline is undoubtedly the change in the position of women themselves. During the nineteenth century the need for a male spokesman to represent them in public gradually declined as their lives became less circumscribed by rules and conventions. Although access to Parliament was denied them until virtually the end of the period of this study, other organisations were slowly opened to them, including the universities, and it may have seemed, to men and women alike, that these changes made male involvement not only less necessary, but even undesirable. It is doubtful, however, if this is the only explanation for the decline in main involvement which becomes apparent in cohort II before women had achieved any real breakthrough into the public sphere. It is necessary, therefore, to look more closely at the characteristics of male feminists in order to look for other reasons for what appears to be their withdrawal from the women's cause.

The male sample, like the female sample, came predominantly from the middle classes, but they were more likely to come from a working-class background. As many as 28%

of the male sample had a social origin that was working-class compared with 16% of the female sample, in spite of the much smaller proportion of the male sample in the cohorts III and IV, which provided most of those in the female sample with a working-class social orign. The men had all, however, been socially mobile.

The next distinguishing feature is the extent to which the male sample were freethinkers. Indeed, as many as 56% fall into this category compared with only 33% of the women. Women were more likely than men to have no known religious affiliation. Indeed, there were no men in this category. They were, however, no more likely to have a positive religious affiliation. On the other hand, of the eight men with a positive religious affiliation, four were Unitarians, a much higher proportion than for women.

It is, however, the difference in the political affiliation of the male and female sample that is most significant, for the female sample, in spite of their higher social class background, were more likely to be socialist. Indeed, only 33% of the men were socialist in political affiliation, compared with 46% of the women. The men in fact were overwhelmingly Liberal, with 61% of the men falling into this political category as compared with only 16% of the women. This does not, however, mean that the men did not share in the move from libralism to socialism which occurred within the female sample in the last two decades of the nineteenth century. If we look simply at cohort III, 80% of the men were socialists and only 75% of the women. Moreover, the only man in cohort IV, Henry Brailsford, was also socialist in his political affiliation. The smaller proportion of socialists in the male sample as a whole, therefore, is due to the way in which men began to move out of the women's movement at about the time when Liberalism was ceasing to be its dominant political affiliation. The inference to be drawn, is that there was never the kind of rapprochement for men between socialism and feminism that there clearly was for women. Although socialism provided some very important male feminists, including eminent socialist leaders like Keir Hardie and George Lansbury, it is difficult to avoid the conclusion that male socialists, in spite of the movement's ideological commitment to sex equality, felt less sympathetic to the goals of feminism than men whose political commitment was to Liberalism.

Male feminists were also found to be committed to similar causes to their female counterparts, especially when their cohort is taken into account. Thus, in the early cohorts, males, like females, were associated most closely with the repeal of the Corn-Laws (2), the cause of Italian unity (2), and Chartism (2). Only one man was involved in the anti-slavery movement however, and this seems to have been important as a way into feminism for women rather than men. There is no doubt, however, of the extent to which the men were touched by reforming zeal. As many as five were involved in educational reform of one kind or another, and other issues included working-class housing and the anti-vivisection movement. The small group of men in cohorts III and IV were also reformers, even apart from their socialism. Other causes included temperance (3) and pacifism (4). A number, like Henry Nevinson and Henry Brailsford, also involved themselves in the issue of political oppression abroad.

The most distinguishing feature of the male feminist, however, is the extent to which their feminism was just one amongst a number of causes and not, as in the case of many of the women, the one cause to which they devoted their lives. William Shaen, for example, although best known for his stand against the Contagious Diseases Acts, was also involved in temperance, the anti-vivisection campaign, the anti-slavery movement, and the working men's college movement. His work for the unity of Italy movement, and especially for Italian refugees, earned him the nickname of *l'angelo salvatore* (Shaen 1912). Similarly, James Stansfeld, for many years the parliamentary leader of the campaign against the Contagious Diseases Acts, was also involved in the unity of Italy movement to an extent which for a time jeopardised his parliamentary career (Hammond 1932). Henry Nevinson was a crusading journalist who spent most of his life trying to help subject people struggling for freedom, for whom the suffragettes represented the same spectacle of suffering and oppression (Nevinson 1925).

Another clue to our understanding of the kind of men who were active in the women's movement is provided by their occupations. All followed middle-class occupations, but in the professions rather than business, and within the professional category the main emphasis was on law, journalism and politics. As many as 44% were at some time in the House of Commons. They were also highly educated, eleven of the eighteen having degrees. Significantly too, it was their professional expertise or, in the case of the politicians, their voice in Parliament which enabled these men to serve the women's movement. Richard Pankhurst, for example, was responsible for the drafts of several bills introduced into the House of Commons during the 1860s and 1870s, mainly on the issue of married women's property and earnings. In 1869 he acted as counsel in a suit in which women's enfranchisement was claimed on the basis of ancient statutes (Rosen 1974).

Journalists also had a special part to play in placing the women's case in a favourable light to their readers, and Henry Nevinson was one of their chief advocates in the years between 1907 and the First World War (Mitchell 1977a). The support of editors was particularly important, and the feminism of William Fox provided a vehicle for feminist argument both from his own pen and from pens of others during the 1820s and 1830s in the pages of the radical Unitarian journal the *Monthly Repository*. An article by Harriet Martineau 'On Female Education' was published in it as early as 1823 and Fox himself advocated female suffrage in an outspoken article in 1832 (Mineka 1972).

But it was as politicians that men were best able to serve the feminist cause. John Stuart Mill, Jacob Bright, Charles Dilke and Henry Fawcett were all involved in attempts to introduce legislation favourable to women, some of which was successful. Jacob Bright, for example, won for unmarried women householders the right to the municipal franchise as early as 1869 (Fulford 1956), and during the 1870s and 1880s legislation considerably improved the position of married women with respect to their property and earnings (Holcombe 1983). James Stansfeld, apart from his work in the House of Commons for the repeal of the Contagious Diseases Acts, was able, as President of the Poor Law Board, to appoint the first woman Poor Law Inspector in 1872. He was also influential in the passage of legislation in

1876 which did much to further the cause of women's medical education (Hammond 1932). Henry Fawcett as Postmaster General was responsible for the appointment of the first woman Medical Officer (Stephen 1886). Similarly, Charles Dilka used his position as President of the Local Government Board to appoint several women members of the Metropolitan Asylum Board (Gwynn and Tuckwell 1917).

With the change from a Liberal/feminist to a mainly socialist/feminist alliance it might have been expected that even more support would have been forthcoming for the women's movement. Although the Liberals had been helpful allies, the Liberal Party itself was by no means committed to feminism, and on the suffrage issue especially strong rank and file support within the Liberal Party was by no means shared by the Party leaders. Indeed, both Gladstone and Asquith were quite determined in their opposition. Disappointment with the Liberal alliance, moreover, was a factor in turning some feminists towards socialism.

Within the Labour movement, on the other hand, in spite of pockets of anti-feminism, like the Marxist Social Democratic Federation, there was a general adherence to the principle of sex equality as a part of the egalitarianism intrinsic to socialism. There was also considerable, although again not universal, support for women's suffrage. There was, however, widespread opposition to the suffrage movement's campaign for women's suffrage on the same terms as men, and a demand that votes for women should be accepted only as part of adult or universal suffrage. Behind this opposition was the fear that a limited suffrage bill, by giving votes only to women with property, would work to the disadvantage of the newly formed Labour Party.

Consequently, socialists, whether men or women, who accepted the value of even a limited suffrage bill to women, including working-class women, were forced into opposition within their own movement. Keir Hardie, for example, fought desperately to get his colleagues to accept the idea of a limited suffrage bill (Morgan 1975b) and George Lansbury actually resigned his seat in Parliament because of his opposition to the Labour Party's cavalier attitude to women's suffrage (Postgate 1951). At the same time, the acceptance of the concept of the family wage led to opposition within much of the Labour and trade union movement to the idea of married women's economic independence, whether through their position in the labour force or through some form of payment to mothers in the home. Instead it was widely held by both men and women that any improvement in the lives of working-class women must come as a result of raising the standard of living of the working-class family. This concept of the family as a unit prevented any serious consideration of relationships within the working-class family and made it possible to reconcile patriarchy and socialism. In 1913, for example, when the Women's Co-operative Guild launched a campaign for the payment of maternity benefit (available since 1911 under the National Insurance Act), direct to mothers it was strongly opposed by the Labour Party in Parliament (Rowan 1982), forcing Philip Snowden, at this time a very committed feminist, to defy the Party whips in order to support the proposal (Webb 1927).

Consequently, although many socialists were prepared to concede sex equality as a general principle, the actual demands made by feminists frequently appeared at best as trivial or irrelevant, and at worst, like limited suffrage, as a threat to the future of socialism. Under such circumstances it is perhaps not so surprising that so few socialist men were drawn into feminism. This is particularly true of cohort IV, which contains only one name, Henry Brailsford. So by roughly 1900 the rise of the Labour movement, while it was, for a time at least, bringing socialism and feminism together for many women, seems to have been driving men away. Men, it would seem, were less willing to try to reconcile feminism and socialism, and certainly far less prepared when the need arose to put the issue of gender in first rather than second place. It was suggested in an earlier chapter that women's attempts to reconcile socialism and feminism were by no means always successful and, in the last resort, distracted many women from feminism altogether, but this was in the long run. The first effect of the alliance between feminism and socialism was to bring feminist and socialist women together, and to give a new dimension to feminist ideology. Male socialists, with certain notable exceptions, far from being drawn to feminism, seem to have found it on the whole an uncongenial ideology.

To note the significance of political affiliation in explaining change over time in the relationship of men to the women's movement does not, however, tell us a great deal about the motivation of individuals. To do this it is necessary to consider the personal relationships of the men in the sample, which were classified in so far as was possible in the same way as the sample of women. As a first step in the analysis, parent/child relationships were examined, but the small number in the male sample and the lack of information in so many cases prevented any conclusions. The number of absent and ineffective fathers and the dominance of some mothers in the household at least suggested the possibility that this kind of family pattern was a factor in the making of a male feminist, but without more information this can only be the most tentative of suggestions.

When we turn from parents to wives, however, the situation is very different and several clear patterns are indicated. In the first place, it is surely significant to find that all but one of the male feminists in the sample were married. This contrasts very strongly with the high proportion of single women in the female sample. Moreover, 78% of the married men were happily married, in so far as it is possible to know this from the data available, and 50% were active partners with their wives in the women's movement and indeed sometimes in other movements as well. This includes such notable partnerships as Ursula and Jacob Bright, Emmeline and Richard Pankhurst, Ethel and Philip Snowden and Nora and Henry Sidgwick. The one and only bachelor, the Owenite socialist William Thompson, drew the ideas and inspiration of his feminist treatise *Appeal of one half of the Human Race, Women, against the Pretensions of the other half, Men*, from his close friendship with the feminist Anna Wheeler (Pankhurst 1954a, 1954b).

If we look in more detail at these husband and wife partnerships we find that although in a number of cases it was the wife who was the active feminist partner and may indeed, as in the case of Ethel Snowden, have actually converted an initially hostile husband (Cross 1966), this was by no means always true. Richard Pankhurst, for example, was already deeply committed to the women's movement when he married the young Emmeline Goulden, and her initial involvement in the women's movement came largely at his instigation (Pankhurst 1977, Rosen 1974). Henry Sidgwick, too, had begun his work in Cambridge for women's higher education some years before his marriage, and it was largely his enthusiasm which gradually involved his wife in the movement for higher education (Sidgwick 1906). In other cases, however, a common approach to feminism drew the couple together in the first place, as was clearly the case with John Stuart Mill and Harriet Taylor (Packe 1954, Rossi 1970). Indeed, as was suggested in an earlier chapter, many feminists deliberately chose a husband whose views were sympathetic to their own.

If, however, the men in the sample did not necessarily learn their feminism from their wives, an involvement with a woman who was an active feminist, whether or not she was his wife, could play an important part in the man's own involvement in the women's movement. If, for example, Harriet Taylor did not make John Stuart Mill a feminist, she certainly deepened his emotional commitment to the women's movement. Keir Hardie too was certainly strengthened in his feminist stand by his relationship with the Pankhurst family and especially by his love for Syliva (Morgan 1975b).

There is some evidence, too, that many of the male feminists not only liked the company of women, but in some cases found it easier to relate to women than to men. There seems also to have been a willingness to admire intellect in women to an extent unusual for their time, which helps to explain their ability to work with women in the organised movement. Indeed their liking for 'strong-minded' women, which was expressed not only in their friendships with such women but frequently too in their choice of marriage partner, indicates that they were unlikely to share the fears of the anti-feminists that the emancipation of women would 'unsex' them. At the same time they were unlikely to be alarmed by the prospect of greater equality within marriage since in the majority of cases a considerable measure of equality was already present. Nor, with rare exceptions, were these men 'womanisers'. Instead they stand out as remarkably affectionate husbands. John Stuart Mill's devotion to Harriet Taylor is well documented (Packe 1954), but he is by no means exceptional and it is difficult to avoid the conclusion that male feminists' marital happiness was a significant factor in their feminism. It is possible that this was itself founded on an earlier attachment to their mothers, and it is unfortunate that we do not have sufficient information to throw any real light on their relationship with either of their parents.

The next step in the analysis is to consider the actual pattern of involvement of the male sample in feminist campaigns. This is indicated in Table 29 which, for convenience, also includes the pattern of involvement of the female sample, already described in a previous chapter.

Table 29: Involvement of both male and female sample in campaigns of the women's movement.

	Male sample		Female sample	
	No.	%	No.	%
Suffrage	18	100	87	89
Education	9	50	29	30
Employment	9	50	45	46
Legal rights	7	39	24	24
CD Acts	4	22	13	13
Birth control	3	17	19	19
WTUM	1	6	15	15
Family allowances	1	6	9	9
Total	52		241	
Total in group	18		98	

The men were involved in rather more campaigns on average (2.8) than the women (2.5) and this probably reflects the extent to which the men acted as spokesmen for a variety of causes rather than devoting their lives, as some women did, to only one. On the whole, however, the differences between men and women are small, and those that do exist reflect the larger proportion of men in cohorts I and II. They are, therefore, more heavily represented in nineteenth-century campaigns like the education campaign, the legal rights campaign, and the campaign for the repeal of the Contagious Diseases Acts. They are, however, represented in all the eight campaigns including, although only just, the campaign for family allowances and the women's trade union movement. It was also worth noticing that the order is very similar for the two samples, the legal rights campaign, for example, taking fourth place in both samples and suffrage heading both lists with a considerable margin to spare.

Another way in which the male and female samples are alike is in the pattern which occurs across the campaign. Of the nine men involved in the education campaign, for example, all were involved with suffrage, six in the campaign for better employment opportunities for women, three in the legal rights campaign, and three in the campaign against the Contagious Diseases Acts. Typical of this kind of involvement is James Stansfeld, the parliamentary leader of the Contagious Diseases Acts repeal campaign. A strong supporter of women's suffrage, he was one of the speakers at the first public meeting in London in 1869, and was also one of the women's most active allies in the cause of women's medical education. A staunch supporter, too, of the campaign for better employment opportunities for women, he was able to give practical effect to his views when he was made President of the Poor Law Board (Hammond 1932).

One of the most notable findings with respect to the female sample was the change that occurred at the end of the nineteenth century when socialism replaced Liberalism as the dominant political affiliation of the feminist movement. This change is also reflected in the male sample. Although suffrage commanded the support of both socialist and non-socialist men, this was not true of any of the equal rights campaigns. Indeed, with the exception of the nineteenth-century Owenite socialist William Thompson, male socialists tended, on the whole, to confine themselves to suffrage, and with only a few exceptions, of whom Henry Brailsford and Frederick Pethick-Lawrence are the most notable, did not involve themselves very heavily in other twentieth-century campaigns. So what chiefly distinguishes the male and female samples is the decline in male involvement in the women's movement with the transfer of feminists' political allegiance from Liberalism to socialism.

If the pattern of male and female involvement in the women's movement is on the whole similar, this is by no means true of their ideological positions. As Table 30 shows, these differences were considerable, indicating that, even within this small and highly committed group, men's approach to feminism was not the same as the approach of women.

Table 30: Feminist ideologies of male and female sample

	Male sample		Female sample	
	No.	%	No.	&
Unmarried women	1	6	27	28
Autonomy	11	61	38	39
Double standard	8	44	34	35
Equal marriage	6	33	24	24
Economic independence	2	11	20	20
Co-operative housekeeping	1	6	10	10
Mothers and children	1	6	24	24
Complementary roles	6	33	21	21
Protection	4	22	7	7
Total	40		205	
Total in group	18		98	

In part at least, the differences in this table reflect the movement out of feminism of the male sample. The lack of interest of the male sample in the issue of mothers and children, for example, and their concern for such issues as autonomy and the double standard may well be a consequence of the concentration of the male sample in cohort I. But this is only part of the truth. The figure of 61% of the male sample in the category 'autonomy' is not only larger than 39% of the female sample in this category, but

is considerably higher than the figure for the female sample
in any of the cohorts. The highest figure reached by the
female sample is in fact in cohort II when it reaches only
48% (see Table 20, p. 79). The lack of interest in the needs
of unmarried women on the part of the male sample also
reflects a difference between men and women which has
nothing to do with the male concentration in the earlier
cohorts. The higher proportion of men in the category
'double standard', however, probably does reflect the
disproportionate numbers of men in cohort I since in that
cohort the category reaches a level of 50% for the female
sample (see Table 20, p. 79). Nevertheless, it does confirm
the significance of opposition to the double standard. For
both male and female feminists it was the second most
important ideological category. Most striking of all,
however, was the high proportion of male feminists
supporting the category 'protection' since this was a late
development within feminism.

At the same time, male feminists were clearly less radical,
as feminists, than the female sample. They were less enthusiastic about co-operative housekeeping, less enthusiastic
about the economic independence of wives, and more
willing to endorse the idea of complementary gender roles.
In fact, the figures of 33% of the male sample supporting
complementary gender roles is not only considerably higher
than the overall figure of 21% for women, but higher than
in any single cohort for the female sample, where the
support for complementary gender roles is never higher than
29%. Even John Stuart Mill, in spite of his belief that
woman's nature had been distorted by her subjection,
painted a picture of womanhood in which women specifically complemented rather than competed with men.
Their natural tasks, he believed, were accomplished by
'being rather than doing' and their chief occupation was 'to
diffuse beauty, elegance, and grace, everywhere' (Kornberg
1974, Rossi 1970). Indeed it was Mill's belief that if a woman
loved her husband she wanted to share *his* interests rather
than to follow her own, an ideal which was in fact realised
in his relationship with Harriet Taylor (Rossi 1970, Hayek
1951).

If we look now within the male sample to the difference

between the socialists and the non-socialists we find that, in spite of the very small number of socialist males, they differ from the rest in much the same way that characterised socialists in the female sample. Support for the concept of autonomy, for example, was expressed by only two of the six socialists, and one of these was the Owenite socialist William Thompson. The category 'protection' was, however, mainly socialist. Most interesting of all was the finding that a belief in complementary gender roles was higher for socialist than for non-socialist men. In this respect male socialists who were also feminists were closer to mainstream thinking in the Labour movement than were female socialist feminists. As many as 50% of socialist males supported complementary gender roles compared with only 18% of socialist females for example, and 50% supported protection, compared with only 16% of socialist women (see Table 21, p. 83). The numbers involved are small, it is true, but the trend seems unmistakable, especially when we consider the failure of male socialists to support the more radical trends in female socialist thinking. Only one man supported the idea of co-operative housekeeping for example, and he was the Owenite socialist William Thompson. Similarly, socialist men were less likely than socialist women to support the economic independence of wives.

If the move from Liberalism to socialism was an important factor in the trend away from feminism on the part of men, other factors, too, must be considered, and foremost amongst these was the apparent success of the women's movement when the vote was won, finally and completely, in 1928. Women themselves, it has been argued, turned away from feminism at this time, and if women could believe in their success it was natural for even the most sympathetic of men to conclude that feminism as an ideology did not need their support any more. The number of men in the women's movement was in any case in decline before the end of the nineteenth century, and although the bitter and prolonged campaign for women's suffrage attracted the support of a number of men in the years immediately before the First World War, they were relatively few in numbers, in comparison with the early days of feminism in the middle of the nineteenth century.

Even more significant, however, was the drastic falling away of male support after 1918. Some men, like Keir Hardie, were dead, and others, like Henry Nevinson, had been attracted by the suffrage struggle rather than the wider issues of feminism. Philip Snowden and George Lansbury were drawn more and more deeply into Labour Party politics, and although there is no evidence that they abandoned their feminist principles—George Lansbury for example supported the 1920s birth control campaign waged by Labour women (Postgate 1951)—they took little part in ongoing feminist activity during the 1920s and 1930s.

One exception to this general rule was Henry Brailsford, the only male feminist in cohort IV. Although his main interests were elsewhere, he was one of the very few men involved in the family allowances campaign and, in fact, did a great deal to get it accepted as policy in the Labour movement (Macnicol 1980). Moreover, in 1936 he became Vice-President of the newly formed Abortion Law Reform Association. Another man who continued to support the feminist cause after 1918 was Frederick Pethick-Lawrence. One of the most active men in the suffrage movement, his abilities as an organiser were significant elements in the success of the Women's Social and Political Union between 1907 and 1912 when his growing objection to militancy led to his expulsion from the WSPU. It was his money which financed the journal *Votes for Women*, for many years the official journal of the WSPU, and he was one of the very few men who was sent to prison for militancy, where he was forcibly fed on several occasions. After the war Frederick Pethick-Lawrence was known chiefly as an expert on financial affairs, but he did not forget his feminism, and his maiden speech in Parliament in 1923, prepared with the assistance of his wife Emmeline, was on pensions for widowed mothers. He also worked consistently for the extension of the vote to all women, instead of the partial suffrage granted by the Act of 1918, and in 1936 supported Ellen Wilkinson when she introduced a motion giving women equal pay in the Civil Service (Brittain 1963, Pethick-Lawrence 1943). His last feminist activity was his support for a proposed Equal Citizenship (Enabling) Bill which was canvassed, unsuccessfully, in 1943 (Doughan 1980).

Undoubtedly many of the men who lost interest in the feminist movement after 1918, like the women in the same position, were motivated by a sincere belief that the battle was now won. Women's suffrage had come to have such a profound significance for both anti-feminists and feminists that even the partial success of 1918 seemed to usher in a whole new future for women and a whole new scenario in politics itself. Indeed in the years immediately after 1918 a series of measures were achieved, some of which, like equal rights in divorce, and improved guardianship rights for mothers, had long been sought by the women's movement, so that at first it must have seemed that women, through their exercise of the vote, did at last have power in their own hands.

At the same time, many of the functions performed by male feminists were now, apparently, in the hands of women themselves. The presence of women in Parliament meant that a male spokesman was no longer needed, and indeed gradually women MPs did begin to take on this function, with men, when they were involved at all, playing only supporting roles. Women also had a voice, if only a small one, in most of the professions, in journalism, and in the academic world. It was not, therefore, entirely unreasonable for men to assume that women were not only now able to work for their own interests but, because they were women, better able to know and understand what their interests were. Moreover, the change in ideology within feminism, with its new emphasis on the welfare of women and children, may well have done a great deal to encourage this belief.

In fact, as we now see clearly, the optimism of the 1920s was unfounded. Women have never succeeded in penetrating the male citadels of power in sufficient numbers to make their voice heard in an effective way. Whether in Parliament, in trade unions, in political parties, in universities or in the professions, men could and frequently did outvote women by the fact of sheer numbers alone. Even in organisations in which women were in the majority, like certain of the trade unions, the fact that men held most of the leadership positions worked always to the disadvantage of women. Women's organisations, it is true, gave women a potentially powerful vehicle, but throughout the 1930s many of these women's groups turned away from feminism. A particularly significant example of this tendency was the transfer of the strongly feminist National Union of Societies for Equal Citizenship into the largely non-political Towns-women's Guilds (Stott 1978).

Even more damaging to the feminist cause was the tendency of those women who did reach positions of power to reject feminist policies, a point which has been driven home in recent years by the premiership of Margaret Thatcher. One lesson that might be drawn from this experience is that a male feminist may be of more use to women in a position of power than a women who is indifferent, if not actually hostile, to the needs of women in general. The fact that men in power are so rarely feminists tends to obscure this point and there is a tendency to assume that it is sufficient in itself to replace men by women, and certainly there is evidence in this study that women are more likely than men to accept feminist principles and to work actively for them. On the other hand it must also be accepted that the failure of women in power to use their position to promote the cause of feminism has itself contributed to the weaknesses of feminism both in the past and, indeed, to some extent also, at the present day.

One reason for the disappointing performance of women in power has of course been their isolation from other women. Frequently alone, they need to rely for support wholly on male colleagues who are themselves rarely sympathetic to feminist ideas, and it would not be at all unreasonable to argue that only those women who are prepared to compromise their feminism or, possibly, who were never feminist in the first place, who are able to command sufficient confidence from the men that surround them to rise to power at all. Another factor has been the conflict which women experience between their feminism and other possibly conflicting ideologies, of which socialism is by far the most important. The tensions between socialism and feminism have been elaborated at several points in this and preceding chapters and need not be repeated here.

They have been strong enough, however, not only to change the nature of feminist ideology in several very significant ways, but also to draw numbers of women away from feminism altogether.

So it is difficult to sustain the argument that after 1918 feminists no longer needed the support and assistance of men. While institutional power was, as indeed it still is, in the hands of men, women still needed male sponsorship, whether in the sphere of government or elsewhere, and it does not help the cause of feminism if the women they sponsor are not feminists themselves. Yet it is likely that only men sympathetic to feminism will sponsor women known to favour feminist policies, especially when such policies are in some sense in opposition to what are perceived to be male interests. It is useful, therefore, to look at some of the reasons why men are prepared to come out in active support of feminist principles, even when that support may appear to be against their own interests as men.

Men, it would seem from this study, can be persuaded to support feminism out of compassion for women as victims, or when the issue appears to them to be a matter of justice. They are, however, also prepared to support feminist causes when these causes are also their own, a situation which arises because men, in spite of some feminist thinking, are not a single group but are frequently divided amongst themselves. It is this division amongst men which provides feminists with allies amongst those men who are prepared to be, for their own reasons, 'traitors to the masculine cause' (Strauss 1982).

One of the best examples of an alliance between male and female feminists to be derived from this study is the campaign against the Contagious Diseases Acts. Although some of the men involved in this campaign were feminists and opposed the Acts on strictly feminist principles, many others, even if they appreciated the injustice to women contained in the Acts' provisions, were principally concerned by the threat to morality which the Acts provided. Such men saw the Acts as nothing more than a licence to sin, since their aim was to ensure that prostitutes were 'clean', an aim which, if it could succeed, would remove a very potent punishment for male licentiousness. Moreover, behind the Acts was the implication that prostitution, although an evil, was an absolutely necessary one, an assumption which many men, as well as women, regarded with horror and detestation. The fight against the Acts, therefore, although a vital aspect of nineteenth-century feminism, as previous chapters have clearly shown, was by no means only either a feminist or even a woman's struggle. Although women formed a significant part of it, it was also a struggle between men (McHugh 1980).

Although the example of the Contagious Diseases Acts is a particularly telling one, it is also true that throughout virtually the whole period of 'first-wave' feminism many men who have supported feminism, and particularly the claim for women's suffrage, have done so not simply out of compassion or even a belief in justice, important as these sentiments were, but out of a conviction that women would have a humanising and civilising effect on social and political life (Strauss 1982). William Fox, for example, editor of the Unitarian *Monthly Repository* and one of the foremost male feminists in the 1830s, believed firmly that by denying women education men had crippled not only women's lives but also their own, and that women's entry into a wider sphere would have a reforming effect on society (Garnett 1910). A hundred years later Frederick Pethick-Lawrence took much the same view, anticipating that women's entry into public life would be to the advantage of humanity at large (Pethick-Lawrence 1943).

It is this attitude which explains the support given by male feminists to the attack by women on the double standard of morality. Although at one level an appeal to justice and equality, it was totally unlike the equal rights campaign in that it was not concerned with opening up male freedom and male privilege to women, but instead with restricting men to the standards already imposed on women. The fact that this was in effect an open attack on many aspects of male sexuality, if not indeed on male sexuality itself, did not deter the male feminists from this aspect of the women's campaign. Indeed, some of the most potent accusations against men for the sexual abuse of women were written by male feminists like John Stuart Mill, William Thompson and William Shaen. John Stuart Mill, in particular, raised issues which have only taken the centre of the stage in the modern women's movement, like wife-beating and, most controversial of all even today, rape inside marriage. In an immensely powerful and moving passage in his essay *The Subjection of Women*, published in 1869, Mill wrote 'though she may know that he hates her, though it may be his daily pleasure to torture her, and though she may feel it impossible not to loathe him—he can claim from her and enforce the lowest degradation of a human being, that of being made the instrument of an animal function contrary to her inclinations' (Rossi 1970, p. 160).

Men like Mill were able to write as they did because male licentiousness was not only against their moral principles but, we may also fairly conclude, foreign to their natures (Strauss 1982). They sympathised with women who were the victims of male sexual exploitation certainly, but they were motivated also by an abhorrence of male lust which equalled that of the women themselves. They wanted to bring men's sexual behaviour under stricter control, not simply for the sake of women, but for the sake of morality in general. Strongly dissenting from the view, expressed by those men who supported the Contagious Diseases Acts for example, they argued that male lust was not uncontrollable and that men not only should but could control it in the interests of civilisation itself.

The experience of 'first-wave' feminism suggests, therefore, that alliances can be a profitable way of male/female collaboration. Indeed this small study of male feminists indicates that men do not represent a united enemy. There are significant differences between men on issues of gender as on the other issues, and feminism can exploit, and indeed has exploited, these differences for its own ends. On the other hand, this study has also made it clear that alliances can be dangerous. The feminist/socialist alliance, it has been argued, was in the long run harmful to feminism largely because, in the end, feminism was submerged into socialism until it lost its identity. This occurred for a number of reasons, some arising from weaknesses in feminism, others from the nature of socialism itself, but the warning sounded by the experiences of socialist feminists in trying to reconcile the two ideologies is clear enough. But this does not mean, although some women in the modern movement have taken this position, that men should be dismissed as irrelevant to feminism. It is vital, still, to obtain male support, especially where legislation is concerned, and if men everywhere are regarded simply as the enemy this avenue of support will remain unexplored. In 'first-wave' feminism certainly, men in powerful positions in politics and the professions were useful allies, and there is no reason to suppose that this is no longer true today.

Another role for men in the women's movement which is easy to overlook but which is suggested by this particular study is that of men as fathers. In examining the part played by fathers in the lives of the female sample it was argued that it was not authoritarian fathers who produced feminist daughters, but fathers who were willing to give their daughters the support and encouragement they needed to break free from traditional and subordinate female roles. Indeed this is probably true of any male in a quasi-paternal role, including brothers. Moreover, this study at least encourages a rather more optimistic view than do some analyses of men as feminists in so far as it provides examples of men who did not seem to share that instinct for domination which is part of the upbringing of the male sex in general.

None of this should, however, be taken to deny that the main task of a women's movement is with women. Men are not only less involved in issues of gender than are women but they are also inclined to take a more conservative view than women, especially on those aspects of feminism concerned with gender roles, and with the division of labour in the family. Feminists today, therefore, are correct to place their emphasis on persuading women of the need for feminist policies, as well as on the necessity of women taking action on their own to secure them. Women too must be the ones who decide what they need for themselves. Yet none of this need imply a refusal to recognise the part that men have played in the women's movement in the past, or indeed to consider, or perhaps reconsider, the part that men might play today.

Clearly, an attempt to define men's role in the modern movement is well outside the scope of this study. Nevertheless, it would appear from a study of men's role in the past that possibilities for collaboration between men and women do exist, and that such collaboration might also be fruitful in the present. Clearly, fears of a 'take over' by men are by no means groundless, and have in fact happened in the relationship between feminism and socialism, but other alliances have been more successful, and it is from these successes as well as the failures that feminists today may well have something to learn from the past. The form that such alliances might take is still open, but issues like pacifism, environmentalism, animal rights and, indeed, in line with alliances of the past, pornography and the sexual abuse of women and children, are all areas where the ideological basis for an alliance are clearly present. Nor, in spite of the past, does a new and more cautious alliance between socialism and feminism have to be ruled out altogether. All that is argued here is that men need not be written out altogether from the women's movement.

7 Becoming a Feminist

It is now time to look closely at the actual process of becoming a feminist, in so far as this is revealed in the biographical and autobiographical material on which this study is based. In almost every case at least some information is given on the attitudes and experiences which led to involvement in the women's movement, and this information has been used to construct several different headings or categories under which individuals in both samples can be placed.

The first category to be considered is that of a personal frustration as a result of being a woman. Observations of the experiences of others naturally reinforced the effect of their own personal situation, but only those women reacting initially at least to their own experience were included in this category. Of the sample as a whole 32% were motivated in this way, a by no means inconsiderable number, although falling well below half the total in the sample. It cannot, therefore, be called the major reason for becoming a feminist. Moreover, there was a considerable decline over time, 46% falling into this category in cohort I and only 19% in cohort IV. This seems to reflect the actual advances made by equal rights feminists by 1900, particularly in the provision of better facilities for the education of girls, as well as changes in the law with respect to marriage which removed the worst of the legal disabilities suffered by women during the nineteenth century. The decline may, however, reflect the changing mood within feminism itself. By the end of the nineteenth century many middle-class feminists were turning to socialism and with it, a concern for the needs of working-class women.

In looking in more detail at the nature of these personal experiences, the most obvious is the effect of an unhappy marriage. There is no doubt, for example, that for Caroline Norton, the consequence of her disastrous marriage to George Norton was to precipitate her out of her largely conventional attitude to women and to bring to her a new and painful realisation of the way the law treated married women. It was the separation from her children which affected her most deeply and led directly to her successful promotion, in 1839, of an Infants Custody Act which went a small way to improve the position of the mother with respect to the guardianship of her children (Holcombe 1983). But Caroline Norton was exceptional rather than typical, and in the sample as a whole only 8% of women turned to feminism as a consequence of an unhappy marriage. Moreover, more than half of these women are in cohort I.

Slightly more frequent than an unhappy marriage was the experience of trying to earn a a living. This faced women very directly with the issue of sex discrimination, and as many as fifteen women (15%) fall into this category from both the middle-class and the working class. Indeed those middle class women who found it necessary to earn a living were just as likely to meet with obstacles because of their sex as were women from the working classes. Cicely Hamilton, for example, was a middle-class girl who found herself in financial straits on the death of her father. For a time she was a pupil-teacher before she eventually found work as an actress. Paid less than an actor for the same work, she also twice found herself thrown out of work to make room for a manager's mistress (Hamilton 1935). Working-class women were more likely to need to work than those in the middle classes, and for such women in particular dissatisfaction with the wages and working conditions as women was an important route into the women's movement. Indeed, six of the sixteen working-class women in the sample (38%) came into feminism in this way. Although these working-class women were mainly socialist in political affiliation, this was not true of the group as a whole since the nine middle-class women were largely non-socialist. For these women the way ahead was not through socialism but through better educational and job opportunities for girls and women.

Another group of fifteen women (15%) were driven to query current attitudes towards women, and especially single women, not for financial reasons but because they felt trapped and stifled by the narrowness of their lives. The best-known woman in this category is Florence Nightingale, whose struggles to escape the triviality of her life have frequently been described and were expressed by her most vividly in the autobiographical fragment *Cassandra*, which remained unpublished during her life-time (Strachey 1928). Another in the same category was Emily Davies, who spent her whole life fighting to give other girls the chance for the higher education she longed for herself (Stephen 1927). With one exception, this group was middle-class in social origin. In addition, nine (60%) were unmarried, and as many as nine were without any form of higher education. Moreover, of the six who achieved it, most had to face opposition from their parents. Ethel Smyth's struggles with her father are well known (Smyth 1923) but by no means unique, and even as late as the 1880s Helena Swanwick's desire to go to college was opposed by both her parents (Swanwick 1935). By the 1890s, however, higher education was more freely available and parents were beginning to change their attitudes towards it. It is not surprising, therefore, to find that women in this particular category are found most frequently in the early cohorts and are absent from cohort IV. Nor is it surprising that in the group as a whole twelve women (80%) can be found in the ideological category 'autonomy', a proportion well above the average for the sample as a whole. The majority (66%) were also non-socialist in political affiliation. The group, therefore, may be taken to represent the frustrations of the middle-class woman, and especially the unmarried woman, who felt herself denied the opportunity to use, or indeed even to develop, her particular talents and whose main desire was for freedom and independence.

Clearly, therefore, personal frustration played its part in the development of 'first-wave' feminism, especially in its early years as a social movement. Important as this was, however, it was by no means the only way into the women's movement. A small group (14%) of women were drawn into it primarily because of their involvement in phil- anthropy and they saw women's greater involvement in public life as a way of furthering their philanthropic concerns. This group included Mary Carpenter, whose work for child criminals led her eventually into supporting women's suffrage (Carpenter 1879) and Louisa Twining, whose feminism had its origin in her concern for women in workhouses (Twining 1893). None of this group were freethinkers and indeed all had a positive religious affiliation ranging all the way from Roman Catholic (two of the three Roman Catholics are in this group) to Quakers and Unitar- ians. Moreover, only 29% were in the ideological category 'autonomy'. Although all were middle-class in social origin, 43% were socialists in political affiliation, illustrating the philanthropic element in the middle-class women's attrac- tion to socialism. This group, therefore, presents a sharp contrast to the group motivated by personal frustration.

Yet another group, and for the first time this included men as well as women, were motivated less by their involve- ment in philanthropy than by their interest in social and especially political reform. Indeed, as many as seven men (39%) and 27 women (27%) came from families with a record of radical attitudes and political involvement in radical movements. This includes support for such campaigns as the Anti-Corn Law League, the anti-slavery campaign, as well as parliamentary reform itself. This kind of background, even when it was not explicitly feminist, provided the men and women in the study with a strong orientation to political change as well as a strong adherence to democratic principles, and both of these were important influences in directing feminism along the lines of legal and electoral change. The belief in both the desirability, and even perhaps more significantly the possibility, of reform helped these feminists to reject the arguments of those anti- feminists who believed in the necessity of women's subordi- nation, whether for biological or social reasons. The political affiliation of the family background of these men and women was predominantly Liberal, and it is interesting to note that although a number in this group became socialists themselves, very few even of working-class origin had a socialist upbringing. Nevertheless, their background in radicalism undoubtedly played a part in the attraction of socialism with its even stronger emphasis on the necessity of social reform. It is also highly significant, surely, that as many as 63% of the women in this group had fathers classified as 'encouraging', an indication that the feminism of this group was to a considerable extent a natural development from their childhood experiences. Women like Anne Knight, Elizabeth Pease Nicholl, Isabella Ford, Eleanor Rathbone and Josephine Butler, for example, were extending their parents', and especially their fathers', concern for reform rather than reacting against it.

In addition, from within this group twelve women, but no men, came from homes where the case not only for social reform, but for feminism itself, was presented to them while they were still children. Interestingly, in these families, it was mainly the mother who was the dominant influence, but in four cases the father seems to have been of equal, if not of even greater, importance. Half of these women were in cohort IV, an illustration of the growth of the women's movement. The most significant of these, of course, are the Pankhurst sisters, who were brought up to accept feminism by a father who was as ardently feminist as their mother (Mitchell 1967). Others include Maria Stopes, whose mother was highly active as a feminist (Hall 1977), Margaret Thomas, later Viscountess Rhondda, whose mother, like her daughter, was a militant suffragist (Rhondda 1933) and Ray Strachey, who learnt her feminism from her Quaker grandmother who brought her up (Strachey 1980).

The other main way into feminism was through what may perhaps best be expressed as personal recruitment. This took a number of forms, ranging from the conversion of one spouse by the other to the effect of a speaker on an individual member of the audience. Moreover, it could entail a move from a position of general disapproval to one of active concern, as in the case of Philip Snowden (Cross 1966) or, as in the case of Constance Lytton, a transition from a purely intellectual support to a level of emotional commitment in which she sacrificed her health and was ready, indeed, to give her life (Lytton 1914). In the majority of cases, however, a largely unfocused personal resentment, or a very general radicalism, was turned into specifically feminist channels. Moreover, it can be shown not only that particular individuals played a crucial role in this kind of recruitment, but that groups of feminists formed social networks which served the function of drawing both men and women into active service in the women's movement.

Perhaps the single most significant woman during the early days of the movement was Barbara Leigh Smith, better known under her married name of Barbara Bodichon. Her own feminism derived initially from her father, Benjamin Leigh Smith, the son of William Smith who had been Wilberforce's lieutenant during the campaign for the abolition of the slave trade. Benjamin Leigh Smith was unusual for his time in maintaining a strict equality between his sons and daughters, and Barbara was given a personal allowance at the age of twenty-one as if she had been a man. Moreover, she had been exposed to radical opinions in the home throughout her childhood and had indeed met the leaders of American feminism in her own home. A convinced feminist from an early age, she was still only in her early twenties when, in 1854, she wrote 'A Brief Summary in Plain Language of the Most Important Laws concerning Women'. The subsequent campaign she organised to amend the law on married women with respect to property and earnings may be said to mark the start of feminism as an organised social movement (Burton 1949, Holcombe 1983).

It was her ability to inspire others, however, which was perhaps her chief contribution. In collaboration with her friend Bessie Rayner Parkes she founded what became known as the Langham Place Circle, from its headquarters in Langham Place, which involved a large number of women in its activities many of whom are in the female sample (Strachey 1928). An offshoot from the Circle was the Society for the Promotion of the Employment of Women, as well as the first feminist journal *The Englishwoman's Review*. Barbara Bodichon was also the inspiration behind the attempt by Elizabeth Garrett to break into the medical profession (Manton 1965). Other women influenced by her include Elizabeth Malleson, who discussed feminism with her as a young woman in the early 1850s (Malleson 1926), and, a generation later, the distinguished woman scientist Hertha Ayrton (Sharp 1924). She was also largely instrumental in bringing Emily Davies into the women's movement (Stephen 1927).

Emily Davies was another central figure in the women's movement at this time. Unlike Barbara Bodichon she came from an Evangelical background, and was conservative in many of her attitudes. She was drawn into feminism by her own feelings of frustration and discontent, rather than any interest in social and political reform. Yet she was a highly important figure in the movement for women's higher education. Her influence on Elizabeth Garrett was profound and she was also largely responsible for involving Sir Joshua Fitch in the movement (Lilley 1906). Others influenced by her include Kate Amberley (Russell 1937) and Lydia Becker (Blackburn 1902).

Another rather different centre of influence was John Stuart Mill. This was largely due to his reputation as a philosopher, and especially to his essay *The Subjection of Women*, published in 1869. As many as nine men and women in the sample as a whole were deeply influenced by him, either personally or by his writings, including the South African writer Olive Schreiner (First and Scott 1980). It was probably amongst men, however, that his influence was most felt. Male feminists like Henry Sidgwick, Henry Fawcett, Sir Charles Dilke and Charles Drysdale must all be numbered amongst his followers, and during the 1860s and 1870s he was the greatest single influence in persuading men to be feminists. The women who read Mill were more likely to find that he provided them with a philosophical justification for their discontent (Swanwick 1935). At the personal level John Stuart Mill was less successful since he was inclined to be authoritarian and his intervention in the affairs of the suffrage movement sometimes led to friction. He was, for example, one of those who opposed the association of women's suffrage leaders with the campaign against the Contagious Diseases Acts, on the grounds that it would be harmful to the suffrage campaign (Caine 1978). His reputation gave him a hearing in Parliament, which was important for the young suffrage movement, and the wide circulation of *The Subjection of Women* also gave him considerable significance as a propagandist.

Personal influence and personal recruitment was also an important source of feminism even before the start of the organised movement. The Unitarian minister William Fox, for example, not only allowed his journal, *The Monthly Repository*, to serve as an important source of feminist ideas but was himself the centre of a circle of feminists which included such noted women as Harriet Martineau, Barbara Bodichon and Harriet Taylor. Indeed, he is credited with having brought John Stuart Mill and Harriet Taylor together (Rossi 1970). It was through him, moreover, that Elizabeth Malleson was brought into contact with Barbara Bodichon (Malleson 1926).

Another early social network of some significance centred upon the home of the solicitor William Ashurst. Best known for his long association with Mazzini (Richards 1920–2), he was also a friend of Robert Owen and of the American feminist Lucretia Mott. His daughter Emilie Venturi later became a prominent feminist and an active participant in the campaign against the Contagious Diseases Acts. Another daughter, Caroline, married James Stansfeld, one of the most active and prominent of the male feminists during the 1860s and 1870s (Hammond 1932). Moreover, the Stansfelds were themselves the centre of a feminist group which included William Shaen, a friend and colleague of Josephine Butler (Shaen 1912) and Elizabeth Malleson (Malleson 1926).

The most notable aspect of these early networks is their association with radical politics. There are links with Owenite socialism, with Chartism, with the anti-slavery movement, and the cause of Italian unity. It is impossible, indeed, to overlook the extent to which feminism in the 1820s and 1830s in particular was one aspect of a wider movement for social and political reform, in which women's rights took their place beside the rights of other groups which were equally the victims of injustice and tyranny. It is during this phase of feminism, moreover, that male feminists played their most dominant role, and were indeed at the centre of the most important feminist networks at this time.

With the coming of the organised women's movement this picture changed. The women who came into feminism during the 1850s and 1860s were drawn from a wider political background and often had no particular political affiliation themselves. Many of them were motivated by their religious rather than by their political background and by their interest in philanthropy. At the same time, feminism itself narrowed its aims. Owenite feminism, in particular, had been frankly utopian but the organised women's movement concentrated on specific issues and, above all, on women's suffrage which by 1900 dominated the women's movement almost completely. To some extent this narrow focus strengthened feminism since it acted to unite women with very different aims into a single overriding cause. Indeed, at the height of the suffrage campaign between 1900 and 1914 'first-wave' feminism came closer to a mass movement than at any other time in its history. Ultimately, as has been suggested in an earlier chapter, this concentration on a single cause proved dangerous because the successful outcome of the struggle convinced many feminists that the battle for feminism itself was virtually over. The immediate effect, however, was to turn feminism away from the radicalism of many of its founders and particularly from the critique of the family implicit in Owenite socialism.

This is not to suggest that feminism lost its association with social reform. It remained strongly idealistic, as is evidenced by its opposition to the double standard of sexual morality, and for many in its ranks, both male and female, the suffrage campaign itself was seen as one way to obtain a moral and also a more humane society. It was, moreover, probably precisely this aspect of feminism which paved the way for the alliance between feminism and socialism during the 1890s, although it was of course by no means the kind of utopian and communitarian socialism which had marked the alliance between feminism and Owenism during the 1820s and 1830s. The question still unanswered, however, is the precise manner in which the feminist/socialist alliance was forged. Certainly it was in part the conversion of feminists to socialism, drawn to it by the promise it seemed to hold out for feminist goals, but further analysis of the women, and especially the men, in this study shows that it also involved a move on the part of socialists into feminism. The change in political affiliation towards socialism, therefore, was more than a move away from Liberalism by discontented feminists. This was part of the picture, it is true, but there were a number of both men and women who were socialists first and feminists only second. The process of this conversion from socialism to feminism needs, therefore, to be examined more closely.

As many as fourteen women were clearly recruited to socialism before they became involved in the women's movement, or indeed in many cases had even been brought into contact with it. Mary Gawthorpe, for example, was a member of the Leeds branch of the Independent Labour Party long before she became interested in women's suffrage, and it was as a member of the ILP that she was first introduced to feminist ideas. Later she became an organiser for the militant Women's Social and Political Union and was one of its most effective speakers (Gawthorpe 1962). Hannah Mitchell's first involvement was also with the ILP and it was several years before she became involved with the suffrage movement (Mitchell 1977b). Other women in this category include Ethel Snowden, a middle-class girl who was converted to socialism as a student by the Liverpool preacher Dr C. F. Aked (Cross 1966). Emmeline Pethick-Lawrence, also from a middle-class family, became a socialist as a result of her experience with working-class girls at the Methodist West London Mission, and was only drawn into the women's suffrage movement fourteen years later (Pethick-Lawrence 1938).

The women converted to socialism first were, however, mainly working-class in social origin. Indeed, of the fourteen women in this category ten were working-class in background. Most of the working-class women in the sample, ten (63%), were drawn into feminism in this way. It is also clear from their ideological position that most of the women in this group, middle-class as well as working-class, were concerned particularly with the needs of women industrial workers, and they tended to see the vote as a way of improving wages and conditions of work. The welfare of mothers and children was also important to most of them.

The category 'autonomy', however, occurred only once. Nor was there very much enthusiasm for any radical change in the family, although two women in the group were in favour of co-operative housekeeping, and four supported the family allowance movement. The small number (6) of male socialist feminists were even more likely to have turned to feminism after they had become socialists. Indeed, for men like Keir Hardie (Morgan 1975b) and George Lansbury (Postgate 1951) their involvement in the women's movement occurred after many years' commitment to the socialist cause. This was also true of Philip Snowden (Cross 1966), Frederick Pethick-Lawrence (Pethick-Lawrence 1943) and Henry Brailsford (Mitchell 1967).

The manner in which these socialists were drawn into feminism is complex, but the part played by personal influence cannot be overlooked. In this process the Independent Labour Party played a crucial role, largely through its practice of engaging women travelling lecturers who combined socialism and feminism, and especially socialism and women's suffrage, and so brought before a wide audience the message that socialism and feminism were two sides of the same coin. Enid Stacy was one of the most important of these travelling lecturers, especially during the 1890s (Liddington and Norris 1978), but there were a number of other women who were significant in bringing women's suffrage and other feminist issues to the attention of the ILP, including Eva Gore-Booth and Esther Roper who worked devotedly to bring women's suffrage to the attention of working-class women (Liddington and Norris 1978).

Another group of women turned to socialism after many years' involvement in the women's movement. Isabella Ford, for example, was a Quaker from a radical Liberal background who had joined the ILP during the 1890s and later became a member of its executive committee. In a pamphlet written in 1904 she argued that the emancipation of women and the emancipation of labour were part of the same struggle, and that women's suffrage would advance the cause of working-class as well as middle-class women (Rowbotham 1973). She did a great deal to draw working-class women into the suffrage movement, and was also credited with the conversion of Ethel Snowden to feminism. Both Richard and Emmeline Pankhurst also turned away from a Liberal background, deeply disappointed by its record with respect to women's suffrage and other feminist issues, and joined the Independent Labour Party in 1894, although Emmeline was later to leave it out of the same sense of disappointment, and she ended her life in the Conservative Party (Mitchell 1967).

It was, however, during the period of the militant suffrage campaign that personal influence reached its height. Although a number of women played their part at this time in drawing recruits into feminism in unprecedented numbers, it was Emmeline Pankhurst and her daughter Christabel who were the chief inspiration behind the militant movement. Christabel, beautiful and eloquent, was perhaps the most influential of all, and is credited with having dazzled two of the most important male feminists connected with militancy, Frederick Pethick-Lawrence and Henry Nevinson (Mitchell 1977a). Amongst the women who followed her with absolute devotion the chief place must go to her lieutenant Annie Kenney (Kenney 1924) who was herself a very successful advocate for the cause. Emmeline Pankhurst, although possesssing different qualities, was also spell-binding as a speaker, and it was she, for example, who persuaded the composer Ethel Smyth to sacrifice two years of her life to the suffrage movement (Smyth 1933). Nor was the younger sister Sylvia without charismatic qualities of her own, drawing around her ranks of working-class supporters in the East End of London as well as the admiration of male feminists like Henry Nevinson and Keir Hardie (Pankhurst 1977).

It is time now to attempt to summarise the main findings in this chapter so far. Personal frustration on the one hand, and a radical Liberal background on the other, are both significant and largely independent factors in becoming a feminist, and both together account for more than half the sample. On the other hand, both these routes into feminism often needed the precipitating factor of a personal contact to bring a woman or man into active involvement in the women's movement. Particular individuals like Barbara Bodichon and, at a later stage, Christabel Pankhurst, played an important role here and so, in a very different way, did John Stuart Mill. Moreover, once a group was formed around an individual it acted as a focus, drawing other men and women towards it. Feminism as a social movement, therefore, must be seen on one level as a network of such groups from which in their turn the organisations of the movement sprang.

On the other hand, although many drawn into these networks were sympathetically disposed to feminism, others were not. Ethel Smyth, for example, had been exposed to feminism as early as the 1880s, but at that time was totally indifferent to the feminist argument. In 1910 she heard Emmeline Pankhurst speak and was swept off her feet, to devote the following two years entirely to the suffrage movement (St John 1959). Philip Snowden was also indifferent, if not indeed hostile, to feminism until he was converted by his wife Ethel and her friends Isabella and Bessie Ford (Cross 1966).

Another factor in recruitment to feminism which is hard to tie down but is nevertheless of great significance is the spread of information. Feminist journals have clearly played a part throughout the whole of the period, not only as a source of propaganda, but as a way of bringing people together. The story is well known, for example, of the way that Jessie Boucherett was brought into the movement when she saw a copy of the *Englishwoman's Journal* and hurried to the office in London to offer to help with its work (Strachey 1928). The treatment of the women's movement by the press in general is another factor in drawing women into the work of the movement, and the publicity which attended the militant campaign, especially in its early years, brought the suffrage issue not only out into the open but into the limelight. For the next few years it was impossible to be unaware of the arguments for and against women's suffrage, and the response from women turned the suffrage campaign from a small pressure group involved mainly in parliamentary lobbying into what was effectively a mass movement.

During this period women and men were stirred not only by the intellectual arguments put forward but even more, perhaps, by the emotional impact of the struggle itself. The arrests and imprisonment, the hunger strikes, and above all the forcible feeding, gave to those who suffered these horrors the dignity of martyrs and, far from deterring others, encouraged more women to follow their example. Lady Constance Lytton, for example, was determined to suffer with everyone else and disguised herself in order to avoid the privileged treatment that her social position obtained for her. The contrast between the treatment she received in her own name and in her disguise made effective propaganda for the suffrage cause (Lytton 1914), and even the fact that it left her health permanently impaired added a fresh dimension to her sufferings.

Certainly the behaviour of the militants could draw down upon them antagonism as well as support, and after 1912 in particular the escalation of violence began to be counter-productive, but it was largely the Women's Social and Political Union which suffered from this rather than the cause of suffrage itself. Moreover, the constitutional wing of the suffrage campaign was itself re-vitalised by the activities of the militants and it too entered a new phase in which processions, open-air lectures and mass meetings replaced the small-scale activities of the 1880s und 1890s.

This phase of 'first-wave' feminism was halted, first by the outbreak of war in 1914, which brought militancy to an end, and then, in 1918 and even more firmly in 1928, by the final achievement of adult suffrage which brought to an end not only the suffrage campaign but, as previous chapters have argued, 'first-wave' feminism itself.

At first, however, things looked far from bleak. Although some of the suffrage leaders left the women's movement altogether, including the Pankhursts, the constitutional wing of the movement, renamed the National Union of Societies for Equal Citizenship, remained. It was a significant focal point for feminist lobbying, and was successful in achieving a number of long-term feminist goals (Strachey 1936). Moreover, it brought together a group of women who were largely responsible for some of the attempts to create a 'new feminism' designed to meet the needs of women in the future, and which focused, in particular, on the new strategy of family allowances (Lewis 1973). But by the 1930s the feminist NUSEC itself had been metamorphised into the non-feminist Townswomen's Guild (Stott 1978).

Another, and to some extent rival, network was centred around the figure of Lady Rhondda. Owner and later editor of *Time and Tide*, she gathered around her not only feminists of an older generation like Elizabeth Robins but new recruits like Vera Brittain and Winifred Holtby. This network, too, however, did not last long. Lady Rhondda lost her interest in feminism and *Time and Tide* gradually ceased to be a vehicle for feminist ideas (Spender 1984). Individual writers, like Vera Brittain for example, did not cease to be feminist in their ideas, but the significant focus of the group was gone.

By the 1930s, therefore, the main feminist networks had largely broken down. Some pressure groups remained and, indeed, a number of new ones were founded during both the 1930s and the 1940s (Doughan 1980, Smith 1981), but they remained small and in most cases ineffective. It has been suggested in earlier chapters that in order to understand what happened to feminism in the 1930s it is necessary to take into account the mood within the women's movement once adult suffrage was finally won in 1928. Believing that the battle was virtually over, many feminist leaders turned to other issues, and especially perhaps to pacifism. Many of the feminists in the sample were also pacifists, and during the 1930s in particular pacifism began to take priority not only for an older generation of feminists, but for young women like Dora Russell who was born just too late to fit into the last generation in this study. Indeed, it was mainly the failure to recruit a new generation of feminist leaders which produced the decline in feminist activity which started in the 1930s and, in spite of a renewal of interest during the war years (Smith 1981), lasted until the 1960s. It is worth while, therefore, to look more closely at this decline of interest in feminism in the light of what has been learnt in this chapter about the process of becoming a feminist.

One of the first routes into feminism to be examined in this chapter was personal bitterness or frustration, which drove a high proportion of women in cohort I to the actual creation of a woman's movement. This particular route was, however, already rare by cohort IV and the suggestion was made that by the end of the nineteenth century some of the worst abuses suffered, or at least perceived to be suffered, by both married and unmarried middle-class women had been ended, some by the actions of the feminists themselves. This process continued into the twentieth century and by the 1930s it is not altogether surprising if feminism as a cause seemed less urgent, especially to those women who remembered what conditions had been like in the past. Even in cohort III middle-class women had started to turn aside from the problems faced by women of their own class, and to concern themselves with the wrongs of working-class women.

This is not to imply that opportunities, even for middle-class girls, were equal either in education or, even more emphatically, in the field of employment, and certainly issues like equal pay and the marriage bar remained feminist issues throughout the whole period of 'first-wave' feminism and beyond. They tended, however, to divide feminists rather than unite them, as the disputes in the ranks of the National Union of Societies for Equal Citizenship in the 1920s makes abundantly clear (Lewis 1973). Perhaps the most violent opposition occurred with respect to protective legislation (Banks 1981), but the issue of equal pay also aroused controversy when it challenged so obviously the widely accepted doctrine of the family wage. Even within the family allowance movement it was believed that equal pay would entail an injustice to the family until a system of family allowances had been achieved (Rathbone 1924, Royden 1917).

A second factor in becoming a feminist was a background in Liberal politics. By the 1930s, however, the kind of Liberal political attitudes which had inspired many in the first and second generation of feminists had long gone, their place taken by socialism. But as previous chapters have argued, in spite of its ideology of sex equality, twentieth-century socialism, whether in Britain or in the rest of Europe, and whether Marxist or non-Marxist in inspiration, has *in practice* been less sympathetic to feminism than nineteenth-century Liberalism. Socialists of the left and right have tended to see issues of gender as a distraction and possibly a dangerous one in the context of what was seen as essentially a working-class struggle. A socialist upbringing, therefore, may well have influenced daughters away from feminism.

Less easy to explain is the failure of feminist mothers to produce feminist daughters. This had been an important route to feminism, especially in cohort IV, and it might have been expected that as the feminist movement expanded the numbers of women who entered feminism by this route would have increased. It was, however, the women born between approximately 1900 and 1930 who represent what we might call the 'missing generation' of feminists. Undoubtedly the reason for this lies in the decline of feminism itself. These women were themselves too young to have taken part in the suffrage struggle itself and would have reached adulthood at a time when many in their mothers' generation believed that the battle had been fought and won. For those growing up in the 1920s and 1930s in particular, other issues such as unemployment and the threat of war might well have seemed more urgent. Moreover, this would have applied particularly strongly to those from the middle classes who had been brought up in a tradition of feminism which was largely philanthropic.

At the same time, those women who, for whatever reason, identified themselves as feminists would have found themselves increasingly isolated. Feminist organisations were at their weakest and there was an absence of those feminist networks which, it has been argued, played such an important role throughout the whole of 'first-wave' feminism. Instead the 1940s and 1950s in particular saw a reaction against feminism which expressed itself in a wide variety of ways (Wilson 1980). It was not that feminists or feminism did not exist during these years, but that it was largely unorganised and undirected.

It is now possible to see more clearly that feminism as a social movement did not really come to an end in the 1930s. It dwindled in size and significance, it is true, but it never completely disappeared. Moreover, even during the years of decline it achieved a number of legal and other changes which had been long sought after (Doughan 1980). What was most lacking during these years was that sense of unity, and indeed of identity, which was characteristic of 'first-wave' feminism during the nineteenth century. Although the women's movement at this time can be analysed in terms of its several campaigns, as indeed was done in Chapter 4, there is little doubt that, in the minds of the women's movement, these campaigns were all part of a single cause. Even a campaign as controversial as that against the Contagious Diseases Acts did not stand alone but had very close links with the rest of the women's movement and, even though many women felt the need to avoid a public commitment to its cause, the numbers of feminists actually opposed to the campaign was very small indeed.

By the 1930s, however, the women's movement was deeply divided, not simply on tactics, which was no new experience, but on vital issues of principle. Even in the nineteenth century, of course, there were differences within feminism reflecting different intellectual traditions, and indeed different religious and political allegiances, but the findings from previous chapters have indicated the extent to which women from different backgrounds and with different attitudes have worked together in the several campaigns that made up nineteenth-century feminism. In the twentieth century feminism became divided, as class began to rival gender as the organising principle behind feminist ideology.

At the same time, the mood of feminism changed. This was mainly the consequence of the actual achievements of the women's movement and it produced, in a whole generation, the belief that the tide had at last turned in favour of women. Under the influence of this mood it was easy for feminists to give issues of gender a low priority and to turn to other causes and other movements. Perhaps, indeed, this was an inevitable outcome of the hopes that earlier generations of feminists, both male and female, had placed on the granting of women's suffrage. Although the suffrage campaign did not encompass the whole of 'first-wave' feminism there is no doubt that it was at its very heart, not simply as a matter of justice but as the way to actually transfer power to women. In the 1920s and 1930s, therefore, many feminists did indeed believe that women's destiny was at last in their own hands.

An analysis of the reasons for the rise of the new women's movement in the 1960s is well outside the scope of this study. It seems clear, however, that in a number of ways

conditions were more favourable for the rise of a strong
feminist movement than at any time since the suffrage
campaign. Changes in employment patterns and, perhaps
even more significantly, in the family itself challenged the
ideology of the male breadwinner which had dominated
even much feminist thinking throughout 'first-wave'
feminism. The rise of the civil rights movement also helped
feminism. Just as the anti-slavery movement in the early
nineteenth century awakened women to their own
oppression, so the struggle for civil rights drew women's
attention to the analogies between race and gender. Moreover, as women became more aware of the significance of
gender, the alliance between socialism and feminism began
to be challenged. A more critical eye was now turned on
the achievements of the past and the way was prepared not
only for a new women's movement but a new approach to
feminist ideology. Most significant of all, the isolation which
had crippled individual feminists was at an end. A whole
series of networks, representing a range of attitudes to
feminism, sprang up not only in London but elsewhere,
while the publicity attending the new movement, if not
always favourable, drew the attention of numbers of women
who would otherwise have remained in ignorance of its
messages.

Becoming a feminist is, therefore, a complex process and
it cannot be pretended that this analysis has done more than
indicate the main dimensions of the areas to be studied. It
has, however, established that personal discontent is not the
only motive, and that an ideological commitment to reform
is important too. Indeed, for male feminists a commitment
to feminism seemed almost always to have been one aspect
of a more general attitude in which democratic principles,
a concern for justice, and compassion for suffering were the
most important ingredients. Women were much more likely
to have a personal motive than men, but they too were
frequently inspired less by a sense of the injustice of their
own position than by a desire to end the injustice suffered
by others. Nor must we overlook the extent to which both
women and men believed that an increase in the public
influence of women would have a civilising and humanising
effect on public life. Feminism, therefore, was in part a

desire to redress particular injustices, in part a vision of a new moral world. In this respect it is not surprising that feminists found socialism so beguiling, especially when the new social order it promised appeared to include a new justice for women. In the event socialism and feminism made uneasy bedfellows in practice, but in their vision of a future better world they have much in common

The next and final chapter will try to draw together the various conclusions suggested by this study in terms of their implications for feminism itself. In particular, attention will be paid to the different elements within feminism as they have been revealed in differences in social and especially in political background as well as in patterns of ideology, and the significance of these sometimes contradictory elements within feminism will be further explored.

8 Conclusion

In attempting to write an analysis of 'first-wave' feminism through the lives of individual feminists it was not to be expected that the findings would give rise to any considerable transformation in our views on the history of feminism as a social movement. The details of the various campaigns are already well documented and the particular approach used here has added little to our knowledge of the campaigns themselves. The aim, instead, has been to add to our understanding of the nature of feminist involvement and, by this new understanding, the nature of feminism itself. This expectation would appear to have been realised in the findings of the study, some of which have lent support to earlier analyses, but others have led to new ways of looking at 'first-wave' feminism.

The sample on which this study is largely based is, of course, by no means without imperfections. Some of these arise from the virtual impossibility of defining feminism in a way which avoids subjective elements. A number of individuals have been included whose feminism is certainly in doubt and which some might wish to deny altogether, while others have been excluded whose inclusion, it might be argued, was nevertheless justified. Since, however, there is not, and never can be, any definitive list of feminists, there is no way in which this problem could have been avoided. A number of others have been excluded for no other reason than lack of information, which indeed proved to be a problem even with respect to those who were included in the sample. It can be argued in justification, however, that it does include all the leading figures in 'first-wave' feminism and that its omissions are mainly from amongst the ranks of those who played a minor rather than a major role in feminism as a social movement.

The use of the four cohorts, representing four generations of feminists, was an attempt to introduce change over time into the analysis. Looking back on 'first-wave' feminism from the stand-point of the modern women's movement it is easy to see it as a unity, against which modern feminism can be compared. In fact, however, this study illuminates not only differences within 'first-wave' feminism but even more dramatically the way in which 'first-wave' feminism changed over time not only with respect to its campaigns, but also in terms of its ideology, and, most obviously of all, in the social and political background of its leading campaigners. So it is this change over time, its causes and its consequences, that is the most important and most illuminating finding of the study.

Although there were several aspects of the change over time, including religious affiliation, social origin, and educational background, the most significant by far was the transformation in the political expression of feminism from Liberalism to socialism. Socialism, of course, had always been one of the intellectual traditions within feminism, and a minority, even in cohort I, were socialist in their political orientation (15% of the female and 14% of the male sample). All these early socialists were, however, Owenites, a branch of socialism which was in decline by the 1840s. The increase in socialist feminists, therefore, which by cohort III had reached 76% of the female and 80% of the male sample, had nothing to do with Owenite socialism which was indeed restricted to the first generation of feminists. It was instead a reflection of the new developments in socialism during the 1880s which led to the creation of a new kind of socialism which, while it owed something to Marx, was, in Britain, largely reformist in its policies and, quite unlike Owenite socialism, traditional in its attitude to the family. By the turn of the century it would not be an over-statement to claim that socialist thinking dominated feminism, and the consequence, it has been argued, was both to divide and to weaken the feminist movement.

The main change in feminist ideology associated with the

growing significance of socialism was a movement away from a concern with autonomy and towards the concept of protection, reflected, for example, in the controversies during the 1920s in particular over the issue of protective legislation. The emphasis on the needs of unmarried women was also replaced by a concern for mothers and children. Non-socialists paid more attention to the concept of equal marriage and also to the need for economic independence for married women. It was socialists, however, who expressed an interest in co-operative housekeeping, but they were very much in the minority.

On the whole, therefore, whereas the earlier and mainly Liberal tradition in feminism had emphasised the need to free women from the restrictions which hampered both their self-expression and their development, including their legal, and to some extent their economic, dependence in marriage, the socialist influence was to maintain women's dependency. This was done partly through a concept of the family which emphasised the woman's economic dependency in marriage, and partly by an acceptance, and even in some respects a reinforcement, of her subordinate role in the work force. In both these respects socialist feminism was reflecting the opposition between socialism and individualism, and its fundamental collectivism. Whereas the Liberal tradition in feminism has tended to emphasise woman's right to be free, the socialist tradition tended to emphasise her duty to society as wife and mother.

It is tempting to ascribe this move towards socialism to a change in the social composition of the women's movement. Although the majority of feminists in the sample were middle-class, there was an increasing minority of working-class origin which by cohort IV had, for the female sample, reached as high as 23%. It is also true that working-class feminists were likely to be socialists, but in fact the majority of socialist feminists were middle-class in social origin. Of the 45 women who were socialists, only thirteen came from working class families and, although this tendency was less marked in the male sample, half of the very small number of socialist men were from a middle-class background. The move away from Liberal or equal rights feminism was, therefore, a change introduced mainly by middle-class women. Indeed, it is likely that it was the swing to socialism on the part of middle-class women which drew working-class women into feminism. This was particularly true of the issue of women's suffrage which was often seen by working-class women as a way of improving the wages and working conditions of industrial women workers.

The attempt to examine the issue of religious affiliation was hampered by the absence of any information for as many as 29% of the female sample. This proportion was at its highest in the later cohorts and reflects the growth of religious indifference during the period of the study. Nevertheless, it was possible to distinguish two very different groups, one of freethinkers and one of those with a positive religious belief. This second group showed a very clear association with social origin, which was highest among the gentry and lowest amongst the working class. Religious belief was also linked, amongst the female sample, to political affiliation, with Conservatives having the highest proportion and socialists the lowest proportion with a positive religious affiliation. On the other hand, religious belief was by no means absent amongst the socialists, since it was present in as many as 24% of the socialist women and, surprisingly, as many as 66% of the socialist men. The majority of men in the sample were, in fact, freethinkers, but the freethinkers were, in general, Liberal in their political affiliation, not socialist.

There was, however, no very clear-cut relationship between type of religious affiliation and particular feminist campaigns. Indeed in most of the campaigns studied both religious belief and free thought are represented in roughly equal proportions. This is true even of the controversy over the Contagious Diseases Acts, in spite of the religious motivation of women like Josephine Butler. Those issues which appear to have been relatively neglected by those with a positive religious belief include the legal rights of married women, perhaps because they had a more conservative attitude to marriage, and birth control which during this period was opposed by a wide spectrum of religious opinion.

Feminist ideology, on the other hand, shows a very clear differentiation between the two groups. Freethinkers were much more interested in autonomy, in opposition to the

double standard, and in equal marriage. Those with a positive religious belief were strongly represented in the categories, 'concern for unmarried women', 'complementary
gender roles', and the 'welfare of mothers and children'.
All these categories have in common a relatively traditional
attitude to women, including concern for unmarried women,
which tended to ignore married women in its preoccupation
with the needs of those who were unmarried. Nevertheless,
although this distinction is present, there is nothing very
clear-cut about it and women worked together in the same
campaigns in spite of their differences.

The educational background of the female sample rose
very considerably over time. In consequence some of the
later campaigns, notably the family allowance movement,
were led largely by women who were university graduates.
So far as the middle classes were concerned, therefore, the
swing to socialism took place amongst a group of very highly
educated women at a time when it was very rare for women,
even in the middle classes, to go to college or university.
These were women, therefore, who had themselves
benefited very considerably from the efforts of those who
had pioneered the improvement in the education of girls in
the last half of the nineteenth century.

When we consider the relationship between educational
background and ideology, therefore, we find, not surprisingly, that it reflects the change in feminism itself.
Autonomy, for example, was more important to those
without higher education than to those with it, whereas a
concern for the welfare of mothers and children was
considerably higher amongst those with higher education
than those without. Undoubtedly this reflects the significance of the educational campaign for the early generations
of feminists, and the sense of deprivation, and indeed of
frustration, that they suffered at the restrictions that
hemmed in their lives. The women in cohort IV, however,
although many of them were unmarried, had not only
enjoyed greater opportunities for higher education, but had
also benefited from the expansion in the field of professional
and semi-professional employment. If we look at the unmarried middle-class women in that cohort, only one was living
the life of the unmarried daughter at home, so typical of her

kind in earlier generations, and even amongst the married women the majority were professionally employed either before or in a few cases after their marriage.

This is not to suggest that these women, whether married or unmarried, did not suffer some kind of discrimination as a result of their sex. What may have impressed them even more, however, was the comparison between their own lives and the lives of their mothers and grandmothers, and the extent to which most of the formal barriers excluding them from both the universities and from many forms of professional employment were gradually being eroded. Modern feminists, looking back in the same way, are conscious of the extent to which the breaking of these formal barriers has failed to change the reality of the situation in any very material way, but few of the feminists in this sample, even those in cohort IV, looked beyond the restrictions themselves. This made it possible for Frederick Pethick-Lawrence, for example, in his postscript to Christabel Pankhurst's reminiscences, published as late as 1959, to write, 'nearly all the man-made obstacles have therefore been removed to the equal opportunities for women to devote themselves, if they so desire, to activities outside the home' (Pankhurst 1959, pp. 301–2).

It is in this context, too, that we must understand the increasing appeal of socialism to feminists. Once middle-class women began to feel less sense of injustice on their own behalf they were ready to look with sympathy on the needs of other women. For a time at least the emphasis on suffrage united feminists of all persuasions in the belief that once women had the vote political power was firmly in their grasp, but once the vote was won the way was open for the divisions within feminism which did so much to weaken it in the years after the First World War. The significance of these divisions, however, lies in the fact that they were ideological in nature rather than founded in either social class origin or intellectual background. The move away from equal rights feminism in the twentieth century was led largely by educated middle-class women, most of whom were socialist in political affiliation.

The attempt to examine the family background of this sample of leading feminists also revealed, in so far as the data allowed, a pattern of relationships which was complex rather than simple. Nevertheless certain highly tentative conclusions do perhaps emerge. The possibility, for example, that feminism is a reaction of daughters against a harsh or authoritarian father found no support from the analysis. Much more frequently found was the father who encouraged his daughter in her independence, and even provided her with a role model which, masculine rather than feminine, emphasised achievement rather than dependence. This seems to have been particularly likely to have happened when the mother/daughter relationship was a weak or faulty one, and it is interesting to notice that there were fewer close and affectionate relationships with mothers than with fathers. Mothers, too, were more likely to have discouraged their daughters in their ambitions, largely because it was the mothers rather than the fathers who had conventional attitudes to women. The exceptions were mainly amongst those women who, exceptionally, were feminists themselves. There was also a little support for the view that if fathers were important for daughters, mothers might also be important for the making of a male feminist, and it is unfortunate that with such a small sample it was impossible to carry this analysis further.

If we look more closely at the small group of discouraging fathers we find that six of the nine daughters involved became feminist because of a strong desire for personal independence, whereas this was true of only four of the thirty-two whose fathers encouraged them. Moreover, of this four, three had discouraging mothers. Indeed, as many as eight of the thirteen discouraging mothers had daughters with this drive for independence, compared with only three of the twenty-one encouraging mothers.

Perhaps the most important finding with respect to encouraging parents, and particularly encouraging fathers, was the extent to which they were themselves radical in politics. This applied to eighteen of the encouraging fathers (56%) and none of the discouraging fathers. Clearly, therefore, in many cases the sympathetic attitudes of the fathers concerned was itself a part of the political and social ideology which they accepted, and which they, in turn, fostered in their daughters. Since as many as 26% of the female sample came from this kind of background, it is clearly a very important route into feminism. Although it cannot be claimed that the data on which this analysis is based is satisfactory, there does seem sufficient evidence to suggest that parents cannot be disregarded in the process of becoming a feminist, although the extent of their influence must remain in doubt.

The other intimate relationship with which this study was concerned was marriage. There is a certain amount of evidence to show that those women with unsuccessful marriages were more likely than other women to be critical in their approach to marriage, and an unhappy experience of marriage turned a small number of women into active feminists. On the other hand, for both the female and the male sample, successful marriages were the rule rather than the exception, and men and women with happy marriages were prominent in all aspects of the women's movement not excluding the reform of marriage itself. Indeed for many of them their own experience of an egalitarian marriage justified their support for the ideological category of equal marriage.

More significant than the experience of an unhappy marriage was the experience of spinsterhood. As many as 46% of the women in the sample were unmarried throughout the period of their active involvement in the women's movement and if we include those who married during that involvement the number of spinsters in the movement is considerably higher. The actual numbers varied from cohort to cohort, but single women were particularly important in cohort I, and even more important in cohort IV. Obviously, therefore, 'first-wave' feminism was, if by no means a movement of spinsters, one in which unmarried women played a very significant part. There is also evidence of a certain fear of marriage even on the part of those who eventually chose to marry. Inspired chiefly by the legal disabilities facing married women, there was also a more generalised anxiety at the loss of freedom conse-quent upon marriage, especially when the prevailing ideology was one in which husbands commanded and were obeyed. Some women deliberately avoided marriage for this reason, and others entered it only when they found a marriage partner prepared to accept at least a degree of reciprocity in the relationships.

It would be a mistake, however, to assume that the needs of unmarried women dominated 'first-wave' feminism. Certainly a concern for unmarried women was more frequently expressed by unmarried than by married women, but this relationship was to be found only in the early days of 'first-wave' feminism, and by cohort IV, although the proportion of single women was higher than in any other cohort, the concern for single women was over, to be replaced as a central aspect of feminist ideology by a concern for the welfare of mothers and children. Moreover, even more surprisingly, in cohort IV unmarried women were more likely to support this category than married women. Single women, therefore, played a major role in the development of the new feminism which, from the 1920s in particular, threatened equal rights feminism with an ideology based primarily on women's role as mothers. At the same time, throughout the whole of 'first-wave' feminism, single women were by no means loth to share in all the feminist campaigns, including the Contagious Diseases Acts controversy and the legal rights of married women.

It remains true that single women were very important in 'first-wave' feminism, probably because of their greater availability to serve the movement. This was chiefly a matter of free time, and it is significant that a very large number of married women were either childless or had only one or two children. It must also be taken into account that married women, unlike single women, could only give their time to the movement with at least the tacit support of their husbands, and it is surely no coincidence that such a high proportion of husbands not only sympathised with their activities but openly supported them. Discouraging husbands, like discouraging fathers, rarely drove women into the feminist movement and in those few cases where they obviously did, like Caroline Norton for example, or Annie Besant, the women concerned were of exceptional courage and exceptional ability. The effect of a discouraging husband was more likely, in the conditions of 'first-wave' feminism at least, to stifle a woman's initiative rather than incite her to revolt.

Men, indeed, had an important part to play in 'first-wave' feminism, especially in its early years, not only indirectly as husbands and fathers but more directly, either representing women's interests in the public sphere from which women were still excluded, or acting as sponsors to introduce women into public life. They also gave to' feminist arguments an intellectual respectability which women at that time found it hard to achieve. For the most part these men were Liberals, usually from within the Radical wing of that party, who were attracted to feminism because of their ideological commitment to the cause of political and social reform. Feminism, although attractive to many women socialists, had little attraction for men socialists in spite of socialism's egalitarian ideology, largely because feminism's emphasis on gender conflicted with socialism's preoccupation with social class, and especially with class conflict. At the same time, male feminism has from the start been more conservative, especially in its attitude towards marriage and the family, and this tendency is considerably intensified in male socialist feminism with its traditional attitude towards the division of labour in home and work place. On the whole, however, male feminism has declined sharply in the twentieth century, partly because of the tensions between feminism and socialism, and partly because women have sought, increasingly, the right to speak and act for themselves. Indeed, the modern women's movement has been strongly separatist in its attitude to men. Whether this is the correct tactic to adopt is still an issue for discussion, but the present study suggests that the support of men is not only possible but, under certain circumstances, advantageous. Male allies can, however, be highly dangerous when, as was frequently the case in the feminist socialist alliance, issues of gender were subordinated, if not indeed ignored.

If the emphasis is now turned from the characteristics of feminists to feminist ideology, this survey has revealed not only significant changes over time but differences and even contradictions which have persisted in varying degrees of significance throughout the whole period. These contradictions in particular throw light on the extent to which feminism is the product of three different intellectual traditions, i.e. the Enlightenment or equal rights tradition, the Evangelical tradition, and socialism. Their intellectual roots, as well as their influence on feminism, have been described elsewhere (Banks 1981), but the present analysis, because of its particular methodology, allows a more precise analysis of their distribution especially as it has changed over time.

The equal rights tradition is revealed in this analysis as the strongest tradition in nineteenth-century feminism, at least as far as Britain is concerned. This is reflected in the close association which was found between the early generations of feminists and a Liberal, and to a considerable extent also, a free-thought background. Interestingly, this relationship was much stronger for the male than for the female sample. The equal rights tradition is also well represented in the actual campaigns fought during the nineteenth century and which were concerned chiefly to give women entry into the rights already enjoyed by men, culminating, of course, in the great crusade for women's suffrage. The campaign against the Contagious Diseases Acts seems at first glance an exception since it did not claim for women the right to sexual licence enjoyed by men. A closer look, however, reveals that the opposition was based on a belief that the same standard of sexual morality should be applied to both men and women. Resolutely opposing any view of male sexuality which implied that it was uncontrollable, the feminists, both female and male, argued that men should be judged by the self-same standards that were applied to women.

The emphasis on the ideological category 'autonomy' is also an indication of the strength of the equal rights tradition, especially during the nineteenth century. The most frequently expressed of all the ideological categories, it did not in fact decline in importance until cohort IV, and even in this cohort was expressed by nearly a quarter of the female sample. Interestingly, it was expressed even more strongly by the male sample, and this remains true even if we take into account the high proportion of the male sample in the early cohorts.

The equal rights tradition was, however, no slavish aping of men. The rights that women craved were those that gave them independence and reflected, above all, their desire to escape from the subordinate position in which law, religion and custom united in placing them. It is significant, too, that the second most important category overall was opposition to the double standard, which, it has been argued, was an explicit rejection of masculine attitudes and masculine behaviour. Like the category autonomy, the category of opposition to the double standard declined in importance over time, more especially in cohort IV but, like autonomy, it effectively dominated nineteenth-century feminism.

This domination was, however, challenged from the first by the evangelical tradition, which represented an essentially religious approach to feminism that emphasised not so much women's rights as women's duties. It was, nevertheless, feminist in its outlook and its implications because of the way in which it envisaged women's duties as extending into and eventually reforming the public sphere. Although in many respects conservative, especially in its emphasis on the differences between men and women, in no sense did the evangelical tradition accept women's subordination to men. Indeed there was a strong tendency to assert women's superiority, especially in the moral sphere. In this respect it served to strengthen the women's movement by bringing into its campaigns a number of women who would not have been motivated by the demand for equality. At the same time, however, it deflected feminism away from a critique of marriage and the family (Esperance 1979).

The socialist tradition, in spite of its brief appearance as Owenite feminism in the 1820s and 1830s, is primarily a late development within British feminism. Liberalism was the dominant political affiliation during most of the nineteenth century, and this was particularly true for the male feminists. By the end of the nineteenth century, however, feminism found its main political expression through the various sections of the Labour movement since the Marxist variety of socialism has in general been unsympathetic in practice if not in theory. Although sharing some features with both the equal rights and the evangelical tradition, socialism represents a different kind of feminism from either.

As previous chapters have argued, socialism, as it has developed in the British Labour movement, has two main characteristics that weaken it as an expression of feminism. One is its emphasis on social class rather than gender, and the other is its mainly traditional attitude towards the place of women in both the family and the workplace, which emphasises above all their role as wives and mothers. At the same time, the collectivism at the heart of this version of socialism finds itself in opposition to the individualism which was characteristic of both nineteenth-century Liberalism and nineteenth-century feminism.

The effect of socialism on 'first-wave' feminism was, therefore, quite profound, moving it away from the individualism of equal rights feminism with its overriding concern for autonomy. Moreover, in its concern with the injustices suffered by the working classes as a whole it overlooked the extent to which gender divided men and women even within the working classes. Most important of all, perhaps, it ignored the way in which women's economic dependency laid them open not only to exploitation at the workplace but actually within the family itself. At the same time the whole issue of the sexual exploitation of women was largely ignored. Indeed, it has taken the modern women's movement to document the full extent of that exploitation and to attack its manifestations in a spirit not very far removed from nineteenth-century feminist thinking (Coveney 1984).

As earlier chapters have indicated, 'first-wave' feminism, in spite of its contradictions, was contained as a single movement by a series of alliances in which feminists from very different traditions were able to work together for similar goals. Those who believed that education was a necessary condition for a life of independence were, for example, able to work with those who believed it would make women better wives and mothers. Indeed, 'first-wave' feminism can be seen as a series of social networks linked often by personal friendships. Moreover women, and men too, tended to work for more than one campaign either at the same time or successively. Josephine Butler, for example, was deeply involved in the movement for higher education for women befove she began her work for the repeal of the Contagious Diseases Acts. Lydia Becker, too, although best known for her work for suffrage, was also very closely involved, although herself unmarried, in the campaign for the legal rights of married women and in the Contagious Diseases Acts controversy.

But in the twentieth century new divisions were introduced into feminism as well as a difference in emphasis which changed it dramatically. There were still alliances between socialist and non-socialist women, especially on the issue of suffrage itself, but the general effect of the move towards socialism was to divide the women's movement as women, and men too, to an even greater extent, began to put party before gender. This had, perhaps, its most serious effects in Parliament where, as Stacey and Price have pointed out, women were completely absorbed into the existing party structure which was not only male dominated but 'organized around the disputes of men' (Stacey and Price 1981, p. 90). Women in Parliament have indeed often tended to steer clear of issues that can be classed as women's issues, and women as able as Barbara Castle and Judith Hart, for example, believed that their political careers depended on their acceptance as competent persons rather than women (Vallance 1979). While this is clearly part of an understandable desire on women's part to be recognised for their personal competence, it also, less happily, implies an acceptance of the belief held by most men that women's issues are of less significance than other issues, if not altogether lacking in importance (Rendel 1981).

It is likely, too, that the subordination of women to the existing party structure has been accentuated, in fact, by the acceptance of women's right not only to a vote but to a seat in Parliament. Before 1918 women were outsiders so far as politics were concerned, and this perhaps explains their willingness to place gender before party when the two were in conflict. Once women were themselves part of the political process, with their own political careers at stake, the interest of the party became paramount.

The weaknesses within 'first-wave' feminism that, it has been argued, contributed to its decline cannot, however, be attributed wholly to its alliance with socialism. There were contradictions within feminism between its various traditions, and serious weaknesses within the traditions themselves. Equal rights feminism, for example, depended very largely on the assumption that the inequalities in the relationship between men and women could be remedied by removing the legal and political disabilities under which women suffered. It was this assumption, indeed, more than anything else which produced the over-optimism of the 1930s and led many feminists to believe that on all the major issues at least victory had been achieved. It was left to a later generation to realise that even the vote itself was not enough, and that much more fundamental changes must be made if women were to benefit from the opportunities that the acquisition of legal and political rights appeared to offer.

Socialist feminism was aware of some of the limitations of equal rights feminism and particularly its neglect of the particular problems of working-class women both as workers and as mothers. In the process of redressing the balance, however, it drastically narrowed the scope of feminism by restricting it largely to the concept of welfare. Even more serious was the acceptance by many socialist feminists of a view of the family as essentially patriarchal in its functioning. Although there was room within socialism for a revolutionary theory of the family which incorporated both an end to the domestic slavery of housework and childcare on the one hand, and the economic dependence of a wife on her husband on the other, these remained the views of only a small minority of feminists.

The evangelical tradition within feminism is also marked by a very conservative attitude to the family as well as by a view of women which emphasises their duties as mothers rather than their need for independence and self-expression. It has, therefore, closer links with socialist feminism than with the equal rights tradition since both socialist feminism and evangelical feminism believed not only that a woman's destiny was motherhood but that a mother's place was in the home. It is interesting in this connection to notice that, measured by religious belief, the evangelical tradition was a strong presence in socialist feminism.

The social context throughout the 1920s and 1930s and indeed, apart from a brief revival of feminism during the war itself, in the late 1940s and throughout the 1950s, did little to encourage feminist thinking. Women were distracted, during the 1930s in particular, by the miseries of mass unemployment, by the rise of Fascism and by the growing threat of war. There was also, during the 1930s and right through the 1940s, a fear of a fall in the birth rate which panicked the feminists themselves. This is manifested most clearly by Eva Hubback, during the 1920s an active equal rights feminist, whose writings during the 1940s constantly reiterate not only the rewards of motherhood but the benefits of a large family. Although she remained sufficiently a feminist to deplore the imposition of marriage bars, she nevertheless believed firmly that 'the bearing and rearing of children is the finest of all professions for women' (Hubback 1947, p. 284).

There were also intellectual currents unfavourable to women's aspirations stemming not only from Freud but from writers like Havelock Ellis, who combined a surface feminism with ideas about women that were deeply anti-feminist in their content and even more in their implications (Coveney 1984). Indeed even the acceptance, during the 1920s, of women's right to sexual pleasure drew feminists' attentions from the fact that the growing sexual freedom for women did nothing to protect them from sexual exploitations and may indeed have made it worse (Coveney 1984).

In reviewing the history of 'first-wave' feminism this study has emphasised above all perhaps the way it has changed over time in response to changes in the social, and above all the political, climate in which it has found itself. It has also had to come to terms with its own achievements, as well as with its failures. In the process it has changed so radically that in many respects it was scarcely the same movement in 1930 that it had been even in 1900 let alone 1830. Nor was the world in which women found themselves in 1930 the same world as in 1830 or indeed in 1900 (Lewis 1984). So it is necessary to ask whether, under these circumstances, it is useful to raise the question posed by this study, of how women and men came to be feminist, if the very term feminist has no meaning.

One way out of this dilemma is to accept that there were different routes into feminism, and that these, in their turn, both arise from and lead to different ways of looking at men and women in society which, if they differ from each other, differ even more from what might be called the traditional approach to gender. All the variations within feminism that have been described in this study, however they are labelled, have in common a sense of dissatisfaction with the condition of women's lives and opportunities, coupled with a belief that women's disabilities arise not from nature itself, nor indeed from any of the ills which afflict humankind as such, but from the way in which women's desires and abilities have been made subordinate to the needs, desires, and interests of men. This subordination of women is reflected in law, custom and also in much of religion and is epitomised, so far as Christianity is concerned, in the myth of Adam and Eve, in which Eve is created for the sole purpose of being a helpmeet to man.

Within this very broad definition of feminism there is room for a great variety of opinions on the nature and extent of the changes which might be needed to end the subordination of women to men. It also allows for different theories of the cause of women's subordination, and different strategies for bringing it to an end, as well as different views on the relationship between sex and gender. Feminism therefore involves not only a critique of women's subordination but a belief, or perhaps a faith, that it is possible to bring it to an end. For this reason it consists of both an ideology and a programme of action.

On the other hand, there are significant and sometimes harmful divisions within feminism which arise from these different approaches at the level both of theory and of action. The desire for autonomy was, as earlier chapters have shown, the dominant element in feminist ideology in the early days of the movement, when women as a group had little or no freedom to direct their lives. As women gained a greater measure of independence this aspect of feminism declined in importance, only to surface again with renewed vigour in the modern movement.

The desire for greater autonomy does not, however, make up the whole of feminism. For some the key word has been exploitation. This emphasis grew stronger with the developing alliances between feminism and socialism and drew the attention of feminists away from the middle-class spinster and towards the needs of the working-class wife and mother. In the process women's need for independence and self-expression frequently took second place to their need for protection. The modern movement has also placed a good deal of emphasis on both the economic and the sexual exploitation of women and has had to face the conflict within feminism between the need of women for protection and their need for autonomy.

Finally, feminism has been associated with the concept of domination. In 'first-wave' feminism this found its chief expression in the campaign for women's suffrage, which was seen as a way of bringing political power within women's grasp. At the same time a new vision of marriage which, it was argued, should replace the old hierarchical structure of patriarchy, was a dominating theme throughout the whole of the nineteenth century. The failure of socialist feminism to grapple firmly enough with the concept of domination as it applies to gender is probably its greatest weakness. It is in this area, however, that modern feminism has made its biggest contribution.

One other finding which has emerged very clearly from this study, and which throws an interesting light on the nature of feminism both as a social movement and an ideology, is the extent to which, in practice, it has allied itself with other movements for social and political reform. Although individual feminists have sometimes been of a rather conservative tendency of mind, the political affiliations of the main body of feminists have been divided between Liberals on the one hand and socialism, more especially the Labour movement, on the other. Moreover, apart from any direct political affiliation, a large number of feminists have had links with other reformist causes. Indeed, a family association with reform was an important route into feminism itself. Placed in this context, feminism can be seen as part of a much wider movement for social and political reform in which the claims of women for a better life for themselves are part of a more general protest against oppression and inequality, whatever particular political form it has taken.

Other, parallel, reform movements have by no means always responded to women's claims for themselves, and the rights of man have indeed often been re-defined specifically to exclude women. Moreover, even when the rights of women have been accepted in principle they have often been ignored in practice. Nevertheless it remains true that feminism has asked for no more than men have asked for themselves, whether what was asked was equality before the law, a share in government, or an end to economic exploitation.

This study has not been able to answer all the questions that it has asked about 'first-wave' feminism. There has been inevitably a certain arbitrariness about the sample and, even more seriously, in certain areas the information in a number of cases has been incomplete. It is a reasonable assumption, however, that these problems would apply to any similar study and are, indeed, an inescapable aspect of the particular method that has been chosen. The justification for pursuing such a method lies in the unusual perspective that it throws on a subject hitherto researched in more traditional ways. It is suggested that the findings described in the previous chapters do justify this, because they allow some attempt at quantification, particularly with respect to the background characteristics of the sample and the pattern of their involvement in the women's movement. Another advantage is the way in which it has been possible to map the change in feminist ideology over time. In this way new light has been thrown on feminism itself.

The findings have indicated, however, that feminism should not be regarded as of significance only to feminists, or indeed only to women. The women's movement has been shown to be related very closely to other social movements and, on this account alone, should be seen and studied as part of the general social and intellectual history of the modern world in a way that has certainly not been attempted in the past. The recent interest in feminist history has tended to be confined to students of women's history, and generally speaking male historians have continued, as they have always done, to ignore it. The difficulty so many men face in fully sympathising with feminism arises no doubt from the intimate way in which they themselves are involved in women's subordination, but this is not a valid reason for their neglect of feminism as a social movement. In the meantime it is hoped that this exercise in historical sociology will be of interest to historians and sociologists alike.

List of female and male samples

Davison, Emily Wilding 1872–1913
Despard, Charlotte 1844–1939
Dickensen, Sarah 1868–1954
Dilke, Lady Emilia 1840–1904
Drummond, Flora c.1879–1949
Faithfull, Emily 1835–1895
Fawcett, Millicent Garrett 1847–1929
Ford, Isabella Ormston c.1850–1924
Gawthorpe, Mary 1881–c.1960
Gore-Booth, Eva Selina 1870–1926
Grey, Maria Georgina 1816–1906
Hamilton, Cicely 1872–1952
Hicks, Amelia 1839/40–1917
Hubback, Eva Marian 1886–1949
Jameson, Anna Brownell 1794–1860
Jewson, Dorothea 1884–1964
Jex-Blake, Sophia 1840–1912
Kenney, Annie 1879–1953
Knight, Anne 1792–1862
Law, Harriet Teresa 1831–1897
Lytton, Lady Constance Georgina 1869–1923
Macarthur, Mary Reid 1880–1921
MacDonald, Margaret Ethel 1870–1911
Malleson, Elizabeth 1828–1916
Marsden, Dora 1882–1960
Martin, Emma 1812–1851
Martineau, Harriet 1802–1876
Miller, Florence Fenwick 1854–1935
Mitchell, Hannah Maria 1871–1956
Montefiore, Dora 1851–1927
Morrison, Frances 1807–1898
Nevinson, Margaret Wynne ?1860–1932
Nicholl, Elizabeth Pease 1807–1897
Nightingale, Florence 1820–1910
Norton, Caroline 1808–1877
Pankhurst, Christabel 1880–1958
Pankhurst, Emmeline 1858–1928
Pankhurst, Sylvia 1882–1960
Pethick-Lawrence, Emmeline 1867–1954
Phillips, Marion 1881–1932
Procter, Adelaide Anne 1825–1864

Rathbone, Eleanor 1872–1946
Reddish, Sarah 1850–1925
Rigby, Edith Rayner 1872–1949
Robins, Elizabeth 1862–1952
Royden, Maude 1876–1956
Schreiner, Olive 1855–1920
Sharp, Evelyn 1869–1955
Sharples, Elizabeth 1804–1861
Shirreff, Emily Anne Elizabeth 1814–1897
Sidgwick, Eleanor Mildred 1845–1936
Smith, Mary 1822–1889
Smyth, Ethel Mary 1858–1944
Snowden, Ethel Annakin 1880–1951
Stacy, Enid 1868–1903
Stocks, Mary Danvers 1891–1975
Stopes, Marie Charlotte Carmichael 1880–1958
Strachey, Philippa 1872–1968
Strachey, Rachel 1887–1940
Swanwick, Helena Maria Lucy 1864–1939
Taylor, Harriet 1807–1858
Thomas, Margaret Haig, Viscountess Rhondda 1883–1958
Tuckwell, Gertrude Mary 1861–1951
Twining, Louisa 1820–1911
Venturi, Emilie Ashurst ?1820–1893
Vickery, Alice Drysdale 1844–1929
Wheeler, Anna 1785–1848
Wilkinson, Ellen 1891–1947
Wolstenholme-Elmy, Elizabeth Clark 1834–1918
Wright, Frances 1795–1852

MALE SAMPLE

Brailsford, Henry Noel 1873–1958
Bright, Jacob 1821–1899
Dilke, Sir Charles Wentworth 1843–1911
Drysdale, Charles Robert 1829–1907
Fawcett, Henry 1833–1884
Fitch, Sir Joshua Girling 1824–1903
Fox, William Johnson 1786–1864
Hardie, Keir 1856–1915

Lansbury, George 1859–1940
Mill, John Stuart 1806–1873
Nevinson, Henry Woodd 1856–1941
Pankhurst, Richard Marsden 1835–1898
Pethick-Lawrence, Frederick William 1871–1961
Shaen, William 1820–1887
Sidgwick, Henry 1838–1899
Snowden, Philip 1864–1937
Stansfeld, James 1820–1898
Thompson, William 1775–1833

Bibliography

Betty Ellen Askwith, *Lady Dilke: a biography* (Chatto and Windus, London, 1969).

Olive Banks, *Faces of Feminism* (Martin Robertson, Oxford, 1981).

Olive Banks, *The Biographical Dictionary of British Feminists*, Vol. 1, 1800–1930 (Wheatsheaf Books, Brighton, Sussex 1985).

J. A. and O. Banks, *Feminism and Family Planning in Victorian England* (Liverpool University Press, Liverpool, 1964).

Joyce Avrech Berkman, *Olive Schreiner, Feminism on the Frontier* (Edens Press, London, 1979).

Helen Blackburn, *Woman's Suffrage: a record of the woman's suffrage movement in the British Isles, with biographical sketches of Lydia Becker* (Williams and Norgate, London, 1902).

Marilyn J. Boer and J. H. Quotaert (eds.), *Socialist Women. European Socialist Feminism in the Nineteenth and early Twentieth Centuries* (Elsevier, New York, 1978).

Margaret Bondfield, *A Life's Work* (Hutchinson, London, 1949).

Jessie Boucherett and Helen Blackburn, *The Condition of Working Women and the Factory Acts* (Elliot Stock, London, 1896).

Nancy Boyd, *Josephine Butler, Octavia Hill, Florence Nightingale. Three Victorian Women who changed their World* (Macmillan, London, 1982)

Esther Bright, *Old Memories and Letters of Annie Besant* (Theosophical Publishing House, London, 1936).

Vera Brittain, *Pethick-Lawrence. A Portrait* (Allen and Unwin, London, 1963).

J. Brophy and C. Smart, 'From disregard to disrepute: the position of women in family law', in *Feminist Review*, 9 October 1981, pp. 3–16.

Joan N. Burstyn, *Victorian Education and the Ideal of Womanhood* (Croom Helm, London, 1980).

Hester Burton, *Barbara Bodichon 1827–1891* (John Murray, London, 1949).

Josephine E. Butler (ed.), *Woman's Work and Woman's Culture* (Macmillan, London, 1869).

Josephine E. Butler, *Recollections of George Butler* (J. W. Arrowsmith, Bristol, 1892).

Josephine E. Butler, *Personal Reminiscences of a Great Crusade* (Horace Marshall, London, 1898).

B. Caine, 'John Stuart Mill and the English Women's Movement', *Historical Studies*, Vol. 18, pp. 52–67 (1978).

J. Estlin Carpenter, *The Life and Work of Mary Carpenter* (Macmillan, London, 1879).

Doris Nield Chew, *Ada Nield Chew. The Life and Writings of a Working Woman* (Virago, London, 1982).

Blanche A. Clough, *Memoir of Anne Jemima Clough. First Principal of Newnham College* (Arnold, London, 1903).

Frances Power Cobbe, 'Final Causes of Woman', in *Woman's Work and Woman's Culture*, ed. Josephine E. Butler (Macmillan, London, 1869).

Frances Power Cobbe, *Life of Frances Power Cobbe as told by herself* (Richard Bentley, London, 1894).

Gertrude Colmore, *The Life of Emily Davison* (The Woman's Press, London, 1913).

L. Coveney *et al.*, *The Sexuality Papers: male sexuality and the social control of women* (Hutchinson in association with Explorations in Feminism Collective, London, 1984).

S. C. Cronwright-Schreiner, *The Letters of Olive Schreiner 1876–1920* (T. Fisher Unwin Ltd., London, 1924). Hyperion Reprinted 1976 (Hyperion Press, Westport, Connecticut, 1976).

Colin Cross, *Philip Snowden* (Barrie and Rockliff, London, 1966).

B. M. Willmott Dobbie, *A Nest of Suffragettes in Somerset. Eagle House, Batheaston* (Batheaston Society, Bath, 1979).

D. Doughan, *Lobbying for Liberation: British Feminism 1918–1968* (City of London Polytechnic, London, 1980).

Edward W. Ellsworth, *Literature of the Female Mind. Educational Reform and the Women's Movement* (Greenwood Press, London, 1979).

Jean Lawrence Esperance, 'Woman's Mission to Women. Explanations in the Operation of the Double Standard and Female

Solidarity in Nineteenth Century England', *Social History*, Vol. 12, pp. 316–38 (1979).

Ellis Ethelmer, 'A Woman Emancipator. A Biographical Sketch', *Westminster Review*, V. 145, pp. 424–8 (1896).

Ruth First and Ann Scott, *Olive Schreiner* (Deutsch, London, 1980).

Margaret Forster, *Significant Sisters* (Secker and Warburg, London, 1984).

Roger Fulford, *Votes for Women. The Story of a Struggle* (Faber and Faber, London, 1956).

Jean Gaffin and David Thoms, *Caring and Sharing. The Centenary History of the Co-operative Women's Guild* (Co-operative Union Ltd., Manchester, 1983).

Les Garner, *Stepping Stones to Women's Liberty. Feminism and Women's Suffrage in Early 20th Century England* (Heinemann, London, 1983).

Richard Garnett, *The Life of W. J. Fox* (Bodley Head, London, 1910).

Mary Gawthorpe, *Uphill to Holloway* (Traversity Press, Penobscot, Maine, 1962).

Harold Goldman, *Emma Paterson. She Led Women into a Man's World* (Lawrence and Wishart, London, 1974).

Stephen Gwynn and Gertrude M. Tuckwell, *The Life of the Right Hon. Sir Charles W. Dilke* (John Murray, London, 1917).

Ruth Hall, *Marie Stopes* (Deutsch, London, 1977).

Cicely Hamilton, *Marriage as a Trade* (Chapman and Hall, London, 1909). Reprinted 1981, The Women's Press, London.

Cicely Hamilton, *Life Errant* (J. M. Dent, London, 1935).

Mary Agnes Hamilton, *Margaret Bondfield* (Leonard Parsons, London, 1924).

J. L. and B. Hammond, *James Stansfeld: A Victorian Champion of Sex Equality* (Longmans, London, 1932).

Brian Harrison, 'Women's Health and the Women's Movement in Britain 1840–1940', in *Biology, Medicine and Society 1840–1940*, ed. Charles Webster (Cambridge University Press, Cambridge, 1981).

Friedrich A. Hayek, *John Stuart Mill and Harriet Taylor: Their Friendship and Subsequent Marriage* (University of Chicago Press, Chicago, 1951).

Lucy Herbert, *Mrs. Ramsey MacDonald* (Women Publishers Ltd., London, 1924).

Phoebe Hesketh, *My Aunt Edith* (A Life of Edith Rigby) (Peter Davies, London, 1966).

Keith Hindell and Madaleine Simms, *Abortion Law Reformed* (Peter Owen, London, 1971).

Lee Holcombe, *Victorian Ladies at Work. Middle-class working women in England and Wales 1850–1914* (David and Charles, Newton Abbot, 1973).

Lee Holcombe, *Wives and Property* (Martin Robertson, Oxford, 1983).

Diana Hopkinson, *Family Inheritance. A Life of Eva Hubback* (Staples Press, London, 1954).

Eva M. Hubback, *The Population of Britain* (Penguin, Harmondsworth, 1947).

Sheila Jeffreys, 'Free from all uninvited touch of man: women's campaigns around sexuality, 1880–1914', in *Re-assessments of First Wave Feminism*, ed. E. Sarah (Pergamon, Oxford, 1982).

Angela John, *By the Sweat of their Brow* (Routledge and Kegan Paul, London, 1984).

Josephine Kamm, *How different from us. A Biography of Miss Buss and Miss Beale* (Bodley Head, London, 1958).

Annie Kenney, *Memories of a Militant* (Arnold, London, 1924).

Jacques Kornberg, 'Feminism and the Liberal Dialectic', *Canadian Historical Association Historical Papers*, 1974, pp. 37–63 (1974).

H. Land and R. Parker, 'Family policies in Britain: the hidden dimension', in *Family policy: government and families in 14 countries*, ed. S. M. Kamerman and A. J. Kahn (Columbia University Press, New York, 1978).

Margaret Lane, *Frances Wright and the Great Experiment* (Manchester University Press, Manchester, 1972).

Audrey Leathard, *The Fight for Family Planning* (Macmillan, London, 1980).

Rosanna Ledbetter, *A History of the Malthusian League 1877–1927* (Ohio State University Press, Columbus, 1976).

Sheila Lewenhak, *Women and Trade Unions* (Ernest Benn, London and Tonbridge, 1977).

Jane Lewis, 'Beyond Suffrage: English Feminism in the 1920s', *The Maryland Historian*, Vol. 6, pp. 1–17 (1973).

Jane Lewis, *The Politics of Motherhood. Child and maternal welfare in England 1900–39* (Croom Helm, London, 1980).

Jane Lewis, *Women in England 1870–1950* (Wheatsheaf Books, Brighton, Sussex, 1984).

J. Liddington, *The Life and Times of a Respectable Rebel. Selina Cooper 1864–1946* (Virago, London, 1984).

Jill Liddington and Jill Norris, *One hand tied behind us. The Rise of the Women's Suffrage Movement* (Virago, London, 1978).

G. Lilley, *Sir Joshua Fitch: an account of his life and work* (Edward Arnold, London, 1906).

Andro Linklater, *An Unhusbanded Life. Charlotte Despard, Suffragette, Socialist and Sinn Feiner* (Hutchinson, London, 1980).

Constance Lytton, *Prisons and Prisoners* (Heinemann, London, 1914).

J. R. MacDonald, *Margaret Ethel MacDonald* (Hodder and Stoughton, London, 1912).

Paul McHugh, *Prostitution and Victorian Social Reform* (St Martin's Press, New York, 1980).

John Macnicol, *The Movement for Family Allowances 1918–45* (Heinemann, London, 1980).

Margaret Maison, 'Queen Victoria's Favourite Poet', *The Listener*, Vol. 73, 29 April 1965, pp. 636–7 (1965).

Hope Malleson, *Elizabeth Malleson 1828–1916. Autobiographical Notes and Letters with a Memoir by Hope Malleson* (printed for private circulation) (1926).

Jo Manton, *Elizabeth Garrett Anderson* (Methuen, London, 1965).

Ellen Mappen, *Helping Women at Work. The Women's Industrial Council 1889–1914* (Hutchinson, London, 1985).

Harriet Martineau, *Harriet Martineau's Autobiography. With Memorials by Maria Weston Chapman* (Smith Elder and Co., London, 1877).

Francis E. Mineka, *The Dissidence of Dissent. The Monthly Repository, 1806–1838* (Octagon Books, New York, 1972).

David Mitchell, *The Fighting Pankhursts. A Study in Tenacity* (Jonathan Cape, London, 1967).

David Mitchell, *Queen Christabel* (Macdonald and Jane's, London, 1977a).

Hannah Mitchell, *The Hard Way Up* (Virago, London, 1977b).

David Morgan, *Suffragists and Liberals. The Politics of Woman Suffrage in England* (Blackwell, Oxford, 1975a).

Kenneth Morgan, *Keir Hardie Radical and Socialist* (Weidenfeld and Nicholson, London, 1975b).

Arthur H. Nethercot, *The First Five Lives of Annie Besant* (Rupert Hart-Davis, London, 1961).

Henry W. Nevinson, *More Changes, More Chances* (Nisbet, London, 1925).
Margaret Wynne Nevinson, *Life's Fitful Fever* (A. & C. Black, London, 1926).

M. St. J. Packe, *The Life of John Stuart Mill* (Secker and Warburg, London, 1954).
Christabel Pankhurst, *The Unshackled* (Hutchinson, London, 1959).
Richard Pankhurst, 'Anna Wheeler – a Pioneer Socialist', *Political Quarterly*, Vol. 25, pp. 132–43 (1954a).
Richard Pankhurst, *William Thompson 1775–1833. Britain's Pioneer Socialist, Feminist, and Co-operator* (Watts and Co., London, 1954b).
Richard Pankhurst, *Sylvia Pankhurst. Artist and Crusader. An Intimate Portrait* (Paddington Press, London and New York, 1979).
E. Sylvia Pankhurst, *The Suffragette Movement. An Intimate Account of Persons and Ideals* (Longmans, London, 1931). Reprinted Virago, London, 1977.
Bessie Rayner Parkes, *Essays on Woman's Work* (Alexander Strachan, London, 1866).
Emmeline Pethick-Lawrence, *My Part in a Changing World* (Gollancz, London, 1938).
F. W. Pethick-Lawrence, *Fate has been Kind* (Hutchinson, London, 1943).
Valerie Kossew Pichanick, *Harriet Martineau. The Woman and her Work. 1802–1876* (University of Michigan Press, Ann Arbor, 1980).
Raymond Postgate, *The Life of George Lansbury* (Longmans, London, 1951).

Eleanor Rathbone, *The Disinherited Family* (Allen and Unwin, London, 1924). Reprinted 1949.
Joseph W. Reed Jnr., *An American Diary 1857–8* (Routledge and Kegan Paul, London, 1972).
Jane Rendall, *The Origins of Modern Feminism* (Macmillan, Basingstoke, 1985).
Margherita Rendel (ed.), *Women, Power and Political Systems* (Croom Helm, London, 1981).
Viscountess Rhondda, *This was my world* (Macmillan, London, 1933).
E. F. Richards (ed.), *Mazzini's Letters to an English Family 1855–1860*. Three Volumes (John Lane, London, 1920–2).

Elizabeth Robins (Anon.), *Ancilla's Share. An Indictment of Sex Antagonism* (Hutchinson, London, 1924).

Andrew Rosen, *Rise Up Women! The Militant Campaign of the Women's Social and Political Union 1903–1914* (Routledge and Kegan Paul, London, 1974).

Alice S. Rossi (ed.), *Essays on Sex Equality. John Stuart Mill and Harriet Taylor Mill* (University of Chicago Press, Chicago and London, 1970).

Constance Rover, *Women's Suffrage and Party Politics in Britain 1866–1914* (Routledge and Kegan Paul, London, 1967).

Caroline Rowan, 'Women in the Labour Party 1906–1920', *Feminist Review*, Vol. 12, pp. 74–91 (1982).

Sheila Rowbotham, *Hidden from History* (Pluto Press, London, 1973).

Sheila Rowbotham, *A New World for Women* (Pluto Press, London, 1977).

Sheila Rowbotham and Jeffrey Weeks, *Socialism and the New Life: The Personal and Sexual Politics of Edward Carpenter and Havelock Ellis* (Pluto Press, London, 1977).

Maude E. Royden, *National Endowment of Motherhood* (Women's International League Pamphlet, London, 1917).

Maude E. Royden, *A Three-Fold Cord* (Gollancz, London, 1947).

Bertrand and Patricia Russell (eds.), *The Amberley Papers. The Letters and Diaries of Lord and Lady Amberley* (Hogarth Press, London, 1937).

Dora Russell, *The Tamarisk Tree*, Vol. 1 (Virago, London, 1975).

Christopher St. John, *Ethel Smyth. A Biography* (Longmans, Green and Co., London, 1959).

Elizabeth Sarah (ed.), *Reassessments of 'First-Wave' Feminism* (Pergamon, Oxford, 1982).

Margaret Josephine Shaen, *William Shaen. A Brief Sketch. Edited by his Daughter* (Longmans, London, 1912).

Evelyn Sharp, *Hertha Ayrton. A Memoir* (Edward Arnold, London, 1924).

Evelyn Sharp, *Unfinished Adventure* (Bodley Head, London, 1933).

Emily Shirreff, *Intellectual Education and its Influence on the Character and Happiness of Women* (John W. Parker and Son, London, 1858).

Arthur Sidgwick and Eleanor Sidgwick, *Henry Sidgwick. A Memoir* (Macmillan, London, 1906).

Harold Smith, 'The Problem of "Equal Pay for Equal Work" in

Great Britain during World War II', *Journal of Modern History*, 53, December 1981, 652–72 (1981).

Dame Ethel Smyth, *Impressions that Remained* (Longmans, London, 1923).

Dame Ethel Smyth, *Female Pipings in Eden. Memoir of Mrs Pankhurst* (Peter Davies, London, 1933).

Norbert C. Soldon, *Women in British Trade Unions 1874–1976* (Gill and Macmillan, London, 1978).

Dale Spender (ed.), *Feminist Theorists* (The Women's Press, London, 1983).

Dale Spender, *Time and Tide Wait for No Man* (Pandora Press, London, 1984).

Enid Stacy, 'A Century of Women's Rights' in *Forecasts of the Coming Century*, ed. Edward Carpenter (Labour Press, Manchester, 1897).

Margaret Stacey and Marion Price, *Women, Power, and Politics* (Tavistock, London, 1981).

Barbara Stephen, *Emily Davies and Girton College* (Constable, London, 1927).

Leslie Stephen, *Life of Henry Fawcett* (Smith Elder and Co., London, 1886).

Mary D. Stocks, *Eleanor Rathbone. A Biography* (Gollancz, London, 1949).

Mary Stocks, *My Commonplace Book* (Peter Davies, London, 1970).

Mary Stott, *Organization Woman. The Story of the National Union of Townswomen's Guilds* (Heinemann, London, 1978).

Barbara Strachey, *Remarkable Relations. The Story of the Pearsall Smith Family* (Gollancz, London, 1980).

Ray Strachey, *The Cause. A Short History of the Women's Movement in Great Britain* (Bell and Sons, London, 1928).

Ray Strachey (ed.), *Our Freedom and its Results* (Hogarth Press, London, 1936).

Sylvia Strauss, *'Traitors to the Masculine Cause.' The Men's Campaigns for Women's Rights* (Greenwood Press, London, 1982).

Edith Summerskill, *A Woman's World* (Heinemann, London, 1967).

H. M. Swanwick, *I have been Young* (Gollancz, London, 1935).

Barbara Taylor, *Eve and the New Jerusalem. Socialism and Feminism in the Nineteenth Century* (Virago, London, 1983).

Clara Thomas, *Love and Work Enough. The Life of Anna Jameson* (Macdonald, London, 1967).

William Thompson, *An Appeal of one half of the human race, Women, against the Pretensions of the other half, Men to retain them in Political and thence in Civil and Domestic Slavery* (Longmans, London, 1825).

Margaret Todd, *The Life of Sophia Jex-Blake* (Macmillan, London, 1918).

Rita McWilliams Tullborg, *Women at Cambridge. A Men's University—though of a Mixed Type* (Gollancz, London, 1975).

Louisa Twining, *Recollections of Life and Work of Louisa Twining* (Edward Arnold, London, 1893).

Alex Tyrrell, *'Women's Mission' and Pressure Group Politics in Britain (1825–1860)* (Manchester University Press, Manchester, 1980).

Elizabeth Vallance, *Women in the House. A Study of Women Members of Parliament* (Athlone Press, London, 1979).

R. T. Van Arsdel, *Mrs F. Fenwick Miller: Feminism and the Woman's Signal 1895–1899* (University of Puget Sound, Washington, 1979).

Betty Vernon, *Ellen Wilkinson* (Croom Helm, London, 1982).

Judith R. Walkowitz, *Prostitution and Victorian Society* (Cambridge University Press, Cambridge, 1980).

Catherine Webb, *The Woman with the Basket: the story of the Women's Co-operative Guild* (Manchester Co-operative Wholesale Society, Manchester, 1927).

Elizabeth Wilson, *Women and the Welfare State* (Tavistock, London, 1977).

Elizabeth Wilson, *Only Halfway to Paradise. Women in Postwar Britain 1945–1968* (Tavistock, London, 1980).

Cecil Woodham Smith, *Florence Nightingale 1820–1910* (Penguin, Harmondsworth, 1951).

Index